BUILDING A
LOG CABIN
AND GODLY
CHARACTER

DAVID G. LUTZ III

CREATION HOUSE
A STRANG COMPANY

BUILDING A LOG CABIN AND GODLY CHARACTER
by David G. Lutz III
Published by Creation House
A Strang Company
600 Rinehart Road
Lake Mary, Florida 32746
www.strangbookgroup.com

Unless otherwise noted, all Scripture quotations are from the New International Version of the Bible. Copyright © 1973, 1978, 1984, International Bible Society. Used by permission.

Design Director: Bill Johnson

Cover design by Amanda Potter

Library of Congress Control Number: 2009932990
International Standard Book Number: 978-1-59979-911-7

First Edition

09 10 11 12 13 — 987654321
Printed in the United States of America

In loving memory of my parents
David and Mary Lutz

ACKNOWLEDGMENTS

To everyone involved who helped, supported, and encouraged me by the giving of their time and talents, I thank you. A special thanks to my friends and fellow writers at West Branch Christian Writers who gave me the confidence to transform my handwritten words from two black marble composition books to the devotional it is today. Thank you.

JANUARY 1
DAY 1

*They replied, "Believe in the Lord Jesus, and
you will be saved you and your household."*
ACTS 16:31

The Idea

Having a cabin in the woods with a fireplace has always been a life-long dream of mine. After I watched a TV special on PBS called *One Man's Wilderness*, a story of a man who decided to build a cabin in Alaska at the age of fifty, I believed I could fulfill my dream. Watching him build his cabin from scratch with no help from anyone else except for the occasional supply plane, I decided that if he could do it, why not me?

When was the seed planted in your life to make a decision for Jesus to be your personal Savior? Was it when you watched a Billy Graham crusade on TV, while you were at church, while talking to a friend or a family member, or possibly while listening to the radio?

In order for my idea to become a reality, I needed to make the decision to take action on the idea I had. I made a decision to accept Jesus as my personal Savior when I was twenty-five years old. I admitted that I was a sinner and that I believed Jesus was the Son of God and I asked Jesus to come into my heart.

Prayer

*Remind me daily, Heavenly Father, to live my life such a way
that my actions will influence someone to make a decision for
You. Amen.*

JANUARY 2
DAY 2

Do not put out the Spirit's fire.
1 THESSALONIANS 5:19

Fanning the Fire

Once I had the idea to build the cabin in the woods, the desire to act on the idea would not go away.

When I received a pair of Carhartt bibs for Christmas, they seemed to fan the smoldering embers of my idea for building a cabin. I now had clothes in which to work out in the elements.

I had the same experience after becoming a Christian. I went to a Bill Gothard seminar and it was during this week that his words blew on my spiritual coals, turning up my heart's desire to please my Heavenly Father in all I thought, did, or spoke. I try to keep my spiritual embers hot by going to church, reading the Bible and autobiographies of missionaries, visiting with Christian friends, and praying.

Prayer

> Dear Heavenly Father, I pray that each day my love for You will be rekindled through Your creation, Your Word, and fellowship with other believers. Amen.

JANUARY 3

DAY 3

Do not come any closer, God said, "take off your sandals, for the place where you are standing is holy ground."
EXODUS 3:5

Level Ground

In mid-February I went out to the pines to choose a spot for building my cabin. I was looking for an area clear enough from big pine trees yet level enough for a good foundation to build on. The site had to be special.

God is holy and He desires my reverence. During my prayer time at church and even in my daily routine my Heavenly Father deserves my ultimate attention. My body is God's temple and should be treated and used in such a way that it brings glory to God.

Just as I took the time to choose a special place to build my cabin,

God wants me to be careful in living my life so I too remain on level ground.

Prayer

> *Dear Heavenly Father, help me to do, to think, and to say all things for Your glory. Amen.*

JANUARY 4
DAY 4

Therefore, everyone who hears these words of mine and puts them into practice is like a wise man who built his house on the rock.
MATTHEW 7:24

Solid Ground

In the pines where I wanted to build my cabin are a lot of running springs. Therefore, in addition to looking for an area big enough and level enough, I had to make sure I was building on a firm foundation.

It is very important that my spiritual foundation is standing on solid ground. Many people try to rationalize their beliefs through man's philosophies, science, and worldly religions.

God's people and member's of God's household are built on the foundation of the apostles and prophets with Christ himself as the chief cornerstone (Ephesians 19–20). Jesus is the one who fulfilled all the prophecies of the Bible. He is the one who has claimed victory over death, and He is the one who sits at the right hand of the Father.

If my spiritual life did not have Jesus Christ as my foundation, my spiritual life would not be able to withstand the storms of this world.

Prayer

> *Dear Lord, I am grateful You provide me the solid ground to stand on in an ever-changing world. Amen.*

JANUARY 5

DAY 5

*Do not be like them, for your Father knows
what you need before you ask him.*
MATTHEW 6:8

The Plan

My blueprints for the cabin, if you want to call them that, were rough drawings that I made in a notebook. The sketches I had drawn out were enough to get me going. Exact measurements, fittings, the placement of windows and doors, and the roof design were not yet known.

When I received Jesus as my personal Savior, God took full control of me and I began a new life. I do not know exactly what God's entire plan is for my life. I do know to try my best to be more Christlike with each passing day. However, to act as if I know where I am going to be and what I will be doing five to ten years down the road would be presumptuous on my part. I will know when I get there. Just as, during the building of the cabin, I knew what I wanted to do when it came time to hang the door, install the windows, put on the roof, and complete the interior, I will know God's will for each season in my life when the time comes.

Prayer

Dear Heavenly Father, let me never forget that You are always in control even when I am not sure what You want me to do next. Amen.

JANUARY 6
DAY 6

Therefore, do not worry about tomorrow, for tomorrow will worry about itself. Each day has enough trouble of its own.
MATTHEW 6:34

How Am I Going to Do That?

How was I going to put in the windows? What material would I use to make the door? What type of hinges would I use? At what angle should the roof be? What material should I use for the roof? I was constantly asking myself these types of questions throughout the construction of my cabin. As time went on, I came to realize that the answers for those questions came when I actually needed to work on them.

I do this in the daily routine of my life. I wonder how different circumstances are going to work out. I ask myself, "What should I do in this situation?" I don't know the exact percentage of what I worry about truly comes to pass; this I do know, God loves me, and cares for me, and promises to take care of my needs.

Prayer

Dear Lord, turn my worry into praise knowing that You are in total control of my life. Amen.

JANUARY 7
DAY 7

For the wages of sin is death, but the gift of God is eternal life in Christ Jesus our Lord.
ROMANS 6:23

Getting Started

I remember the cold snow-covered Saturday morning in February when I got started on the cabin. Like any great idea, it is great only if we act on it. I had to take the first step. This is what I did that morning. I got started by clearing the chosen area of rocks, limbs, and logs, and I tore down the demolished screened-in tent that had collapsed under the weight of the snow.

I believed in God, but I had not yet taken the first step necessary to restore myself to Him through the cleansing blood of His Son, Jesus Christ. In my twenty-fifth year, I took the first step and received Jesus as my personal Savior.

Prayer

> *Dear Heavenly Father, I will be forever grateful to You for taking the first step in restoring my relationship with You through Your Son, Jesus Christ. Amen.*

JANUARY 8
DAY 8

If we confess our sins, he is faithful and just and will forgive us our sins and purify us for all unrighteousness.
1 JOHN 1:9

Preparing to Lay the First Logs

Once my chosen site was free of debris, it was time to set my corner post. I pounded in a stake at each corner. I then took a string, tied it to a stake, pulled it tight, and wrapped it around each of the other stakes ending with the stake onto which I had originally tied it. Now I was ready to take measurements and maneuver the stakes so that my cabin would be square and not trapezoid-shaped. I was ready to lay my first logs.

To receive God's gift of salvation, I needed to realize my need for salvation. I did this when I realized that I was a sinner. By confessing to God that I was a sinner who needed Jesus to cleanse me from my sins, I prepared my heart for the Holy Spirit to dwell within me. The moment I accepted Jesus as my personal Savior, He started preparing a place for me in heaven (John 14:2).

Prayer

> *Dear Heavenly Father, make me aware of my sins and let me be faithful in asking for forgiveness. Thank You for Your promise of a home in heaven. Amen.*

JANUARY 9
Day 9

No temptation has seized you except what is common to man. In addition, God is faithful; he will not let you be tempted beyond what you can bear. However, when you are tempted, he will also provide a way out so that you can stand up under it.
1 Corinthians 10:13

Deciding the Dimensions

How big was my cabin going to be? On paper, I decided that sixteen feet by twelve feet would be a nice size. So when I picked my site, I made sure that it would accommodate my chosen dimensions. I cut my first log sixteen feet long. All was going well until I attempted to drag it to my building site. I could only move it side to side and could barely lift it up besides dragging it. I cut the log to fourteen feet. I could now begin to drag the log, but it was still very strenuous. I cut two more feet off making the log twelve feet long. This I could drag. Therefore, that is how I decided the length of my cabin. I decided the height similarly. Six and a half feet was the limit for me lifting up twelve-foot logs manually. Therefore, the final dimensions for my cabin are twelve feet in length by ten feet in width and a height of six and a half feet. That was all I could handle.

As a child of God, I am grateful that God will never give me more than I can handle physically or spiritually.

Prayer

> *Thank you, Lord, for Your promise to help carry the burdens of life (Matt. 11:28–30). Help me to be obedient to You so that my load will remain light. Amen.*

JANUARY 10
DAY 10

All Scripture is God-breathed and is useful for teaching, rebuking, correcting, and training in righteousness.
2 TIMOTHY 3:16

Books on Building Log Cabins

I had a mental picture of how I thought my cabin should look. One of my favorite toys to play with as a child was a set of Lincoln Logs. Lincoln Logs gave me the general ideas I needed for the construction of my cabin. However, when it came to fireplaces, hanging doors, ridgepoles, roof pitch, and window installment, I turned to books on building real log cabins. By reading these books, I was able to learn specific instructions on completing each of the tasks I faced.

I am glad that as a Christian I have God's word to instruct me. The Bible helps me to learn how God wants me to live my life so that I can enjoy His full blessings. God's word will also help me through difficult situations even when I do not understand the reason for them.

Prayer

> *Thank You, Heavenly Father, for Your complete, unchanging, and infallible instruction manual that helps me through the challenges I face each day. Amen.*

JANUARY 11
DAY 11

Heaven and earth will pass away, but my words will never pass away.
MATTHEW 24:35

Withstanding the Passing of Time

Whether it was reading the books I had on cabins and fireplaces, looking at videos, or listening to neighbors and friends who would come over to see what all the ruckus was about, I always had my eyes and ears open for suggestions. My mind was open to ideas that would help my cabin to withstand the elements and the passing of time. I wanted the foundation to be able to respond to the freezing and thawing of the ground. I needed to attach the roof so it would not leak, and I treated the wood to protect it from rot and insects. I applied all the techniques I knew or learned about so that my cabin would be the same for years to come.

I am glad the Bible tells us that God does not change and that the Word of God will withstand the passing of time: "I the LORD do not change" (Mal. 3:6).

Prayer

Thank You, Heavenly Father, for being the same today as yesterday and in all the tomorrows to come. Amen.

JANUARY 12
DAY 12

There are different kinds of working, but the same God works all of them in all men.
1 CORINTHIANS 12:6

Everyone's Cabin Would Be Different

My cabin cannot be duplicated; it is one of a kind. Even if someone followed blueprints he could not reproduce the cabin I built. It would be similar but my lumber was not milled to size. Therefore, each log is different, and every stone I used for chinking and for the fireplace is shaped differently.

It is true that people are similar. We are all created in God's image (Gen. 1:27), yet we are each uniquely different. Looks, personalities, and physical abilities all differ from person to person. No person can be duplicated; each one of us has a special place in God's plan.

Prayer

Dear Heavenly Father, help me to fulfill the plans You have for me that only I can complete. Amen.

JANUARY 13
Day 13

He is the Rock, his works are perfect, and all his ways are just.
A faithful God who does no wrong, upright and just is he.
DEUTERONOMY 32:4

Keeping the Walls Level

The challenge of building with unmilled logs consists in keeping all four sides level. I tried to keep each layer as level as possible. However, as long as I had another layer to go, I could always compensate for a difference in height. For the lower side I would choose a log with a bigger diameter, or if one side were higher I would notch the log deeper so that when in place it would sit lower. It was the last layer that had to be level for my ceiling beams to lie straight.

When someone says he is being level with you, he means that he is being honest and straightforward. Sad to say, the world we live in is not often on the level. I worship a God who is just (2 Chron. 19:7). So the more I am on the level with others the better will be my relationship with man and with God.

Prayer

Thank you, Lord, for the peace I have knowing that all the decisions You have for me in life are just and fair. Amen.

⚜

JANUARY 14
Day 14

Salvation is found in no one else, for there is no other name under heaven given to men by which we must be saved.
ACTS 4:12

Carhartts

When I purchased my first pair of Carhartts, I turned into a lumberjack. Carhartts make a variety of work clothes. When you dress in one of their products you do not say, "I'm going to put on my jacket or my bib overhauls," you say, "I'm going to put on my Carhartts." When you purchase something with the Carhartts brand name on it you know you have bought a good product.

There is no other name under heaven like that of the name of Jesus. Some day every knee shall bow and every tongue confess that Jesus is Lord (Rom. 14:11).

Prayer

Dear Heavenly Father, I am grateful that I can put my trust in Jesus for my salvation. Amen.

⚜

JANUARY 15
Day 15

Surely, goodness and love will follow me all the days of my life, and I will dwell in the house of the Lord forever.
PSALM 23:6

Carhartts Are Made to Last

Carhartts are made from eight and a half ounce one hundred percent ringspun cotton canvas fabric; the final product is a durable heavy brown material capable of withstanding extreme weather conditions. I can work eight hours a day dragging logs, lifting mountain stone, or any other physical activity involved in building a cabin, and I do not have to worry if my Carhartts are going to be able to withstand the abuse. Carhartts get better the more I wear them just like a pair of my favorite worn-in jeans.

As I grow in Christ, my fellowship with God gets better with each passing day. Even in death, I am promised the hope of eternal life with God in heaven.

Prayer

Thank You, Heavenly Father, for the hope You have given me through Christ for an everlasting life with You. Amen.

JANUARY 16
DAY 16

So in Christ we who are many form one body, and each member belongs to all the others. We have different gifts, according to the grace given us.
ROMANS 12:5-6

Many Pockets

What would I have done without my Carhartt bibs? They played a big part in the motivation I had to build my cabin. One of the features I like most about my Carhartts is all the pockets. I was a walking toolbox. I had a loop for my hammer, a pocket for my string level, a long pocket on the side of the leg perfect for my carpenter's ruler, a thin pocket on the bib section for my pencil, a back pocket for my handkerchief, and a front pocket for my watch and pocket knife. No matter which section of the cabin I was working on I had a pocket or a loop for each tool.

The church has a place for every Christian. Every Christian has special gifts. The church of Christ functions at its best when all Christians are using their gifts to edify the whole body.

Prayer

Help me, Heavenly Father, to discern the spiritual gifts You have given me so that I can use them for Your glory. Amen.

JANUARY 17

DAY 17

Discretion will protect you, and understanding will guard you.
PROVERBS 2:11

Carhartts Help Keep Me Warm

Have I mentioned yet that I really like my Carhartt bibs? When I worked on my cabin in February and March the temperature was often below freezing. I can honestly say the cold temperatures never impeded me in making progress on the construction of the cabin. My Carhartts fit over my clothes, and they protected me from the wind and cold yet gave me the maneuverability to work.

I am glad to have a God who protects from the temptations of the world. As long as we let Jesus sit on the throne of our hearts rather than ourselves, He promises us a way out from our temptation. Discretion and an understanding of God's word help to keep me from sinning.

Prayer

Thank You, Heavenly Father, for the protection You promise me against the obstacles of this world. Amen.

JANUARY 18

DAY 18

*But if we walk in the light, as he is in the light, we
have fellowship with one another, and the blood
of Jesus, his Son, purifies us from all sin.*

1 JOHN 1:7

New Covering of Snow

Throughout the months of winter before I started to work on my cabin, I usually had to clean a two- to four-inch covering of snow off the logs before getting started. The week's worth of snow would cover any evidence of work I had completed the previous week. All the wood chips produced by the chainsaw notching out the logs I cut for construction would be covered. Anyone but me passing by would not even realize there was work in progress.

No wonder the psalmist said, "Wash me and I will be whiter than snow" (Ps. 51:7). Jesus has covered my sins with His blood. A stranger passing by might not take notice of the transformation taking place in me through Christ.

Prayer

*Thank You, Jesus, for cleansing my heart from sin by the blood
You shed on the cross. Amen.*

JANUARY 19

DAY 19

*Let us not give up meeting together, as some are in the
habit of doing, but let us encourage one another—and
all the more as you see the Day approaching.*

HEBREWS 10:25

Preparing for Another Day's Work

Each week I needed to prepare the site before beginning actual construction. This prep work usually included the clearing of snow from the top layer of logs on the cabin and from the tarp covering my tools. My pile of logs would need to be dislodged from the frozen ground and from each other with a digging iron. Also included in this prep time were the sharpening of tools and filling my pockets with the nails and tools necessary for the day's work.

As a Christian, it is very important for me to meet each week with my brothers and sisters in Christ. I need to make sure to fill my spiritual tank so that I can perform effectively the work God wants me to accomplish throughout the week.

Prayer

Dear Heavenly Father, I pray that I get to church each week not only to be uplifted but also to uplift my fellow believers. Amen.

JANUARY 20
DAY 20

So it is with you. Since you are eager to have spiritual gifts, try to excel in gifts that build up the church.
1 CORINTHIANS 14:12

Tools for Building

Here is a list of the tools that I needed to build my log cabin: chainsaw, hammer, ax, hatchet, digging iron, sledgehammer, level, tape measure, carpenter's ruler, hoe, chalk line, pencil, drill, screwdriver, wrench, and file. This was everything I used from laying the first log to attaching the roof, hanging the door, putting up the chimney, and chinking the sides.

In God's toolbox there is prayer to uplift the saints (Eph. 6:18) and there are spiritual gifts to help build His church. The most powerful tool, that cuts deeper than a chainsaw, is His Word, which helps each Christian to grow more Christlike.

Prayer

Thank You, Heavenly Father, for giving me the tools I need to complete the work You have for me. Amen.

JANUARY 21
DAY 21

Who, being in the very nature of God, did not consider equality with God something to be grasped, but made himself nothing, taking the very nature of a servant, being made in human likeness.
PHILIPPIANS 2:6–7

Leaving the Comforts of Home

The work that needed to be completed could not be done from within the comfortable conditions of home. I would leave the comfortably warm and dry conditions inside the house to go outside where the temperatures were often below thirty degrees and the ground covered in snow. As long as there was not a steady rain, I would work on the cabin.

According to God's plan, the regeneration of my heart could not be done from the splendor of heaven. The Son of God left all the glories of His heavenly home. He became man and endured all the hardships of man, even death. God's plan to claim victory over the consequence of sin was completed through the death and resurrection of His Son.

Prayer

Thank You, Jesus, for leaving the comforts of Your home so that Your Father's plan for me could be completed. Amen.

JANUARY 22
DAY 22

*Let us not become weary in doing good, for at the proper
time we will reap a harvest if we do not give up.*
GALATIANS 6:9

Time and Priorities

Without the chainsaw, I could not have built my cabin in a timely manner working only on weekends. Working only weekends beginning in February, my goal was to have it completed by November. I had to use my time wisely. Building the cabin was more important than many other activities I usually pursue. Finishing the cabin was my number one priority.

God has granted me a specific amount of time, from my birth to my death. God wants me to use this time wisely. By keeping God first in my life, He will help me to keep the rest of my life's priorities in order.

Prayer

*Dear Heavenly Father, I pray that I will use my time wisely
and do all things for Your Glory. Amen.*

JANUARY 23
DAY 23

*How can a young man keep his way pure?
By living according to your word.*
PSALM 119:9

Chainsaw Maintenance

Before a weekend of log cabin construction, I made sure the chainsaw was in good running condition. First I filled the gas tank and oil reservoir. Next, I sharpened and tightened the chain. These simple checks gave me confidence that my chainsaw would run efficiently all day.

Each day I must take time to pray and read God's word in order to help me live a fulfilled Christian life. My Heavenly Father will use this time to speak to my heart. This daily maintenance helps me become more Christlike and strengthens my faith so that I can be victorious over daily temptations.

Prayer

> *Dear Heavenly Father, it is my prayer that I will spend quality time with You each day in order to maintain a holy life. Amen.*

JANUARY 24
Day 24

Put on the full armor of God so that you can take your stand against the devil's schemes.
Ephesians 6:11

Safety and Protection

If you live in an area where the use of chainsaws is common, you probably have heard or read about someone who accidentally hurt themselves. It is not safe to use a chainsaw without proper protection and built-in safety devices. I am extremely careful when using the chainsaw. I wear earplugs and safety glasses. The manufacturers of chainsaws have also built in safety features like hand guards, an anti-kickback mechanism, and a chain brake.

Living in the world as a Christian is very dangerous as well. Satan is not happy that I am one of God's children. He is unrelenting in his attempt to break the fellowship I have with my Heavenly Father. I am grateful that God has given me the protection I need to fend off these daily attacks of our enemy.

Prayer

Thank You, Heavenly Father, for providing me with the armor I need to withstand my enemy's temptations. Amen.

JANUARY 25

Day 25

If we have been united with him like this in his death, we will certainly also be united with him in his resurrection.
Romans 6:5

Every Link United

Your chainsaw is full of gas and the oil reservoir for lubricating the chain is filled to the brim. Maybe you even changed the sparkplug and it starts up with one pull of the cord. The previous day, you sharpened all the cutting blades. All of this preparation is good, but if one link of the chain is not united with the link next to it, your chainsaw is useless.

We live in a world where there are many philosophies for living a fulfilled life. My philosophies and ideas as to what brought fulfillment varied greatly before I heard the Good News (Acts 5:42). From that moment on I realized there is one thing that will always be true. No matter how popular I am, or how physically or mentally gifted I am, or how economically well off I am, if I am not spiritually united with Jesus Christ, my life will be useless in the eyes of God.

Prayer

Dear Heavenly Father, I pray You will use me to link someone together with Your Son, Jesus Christ. Amen.

JANUARY 26
DAY 26

For the word of God is living and active. Sharper than any double-edged sword, it penetrates even to dividing soul and spirit, joints and marrow; it judges the thoughts and attitudes of the heart.
HEBREWS 4:12

A Sharp Chainsaw

There is nothing like a brand-new chainsaw chain. I can never get my blades quite as sharp as the day when I first take them out of the package. When I put a new blade on, I can cut through wood with ease. The chips that fly out are the size of my thumbnail. As long as I do not hit a rock, cut through ice built up on a log, or a nail embedded in a log, the blades will stay sharp for quite some time.

God's word describes itself as being sharper than a double-edged sword. When I have my daily Bible reading, the words of God help cut out bad habits I acquired before my salvation. As long as I am in fellowship with my Heavenly Father and do not dull the Holy Spirit's guidance through sin, God's Word will help the new creation I am (2 Cor. 5:17) to become more Christlike.

Prayer

> *Dear Heavenly Father, use the sharpness of Your Word to remove sin-hardened areas in my heart that hinder my fellowship with You. Amen.*

JANUARY 27
DAY 27

As for God, his way is perfect; the word of the LORD is flawless.
2 SAMUEL 22:31

The Metal File

I used my metal file each week to keep a sharp edge on my ax, hatchet, and chainsaw blade. When sharpening metal by the use of the file, all you are doing is removing the major imperfections on the cutting edge. I have worked at a machine shop for the past eight years. I work in the press department. If I do not keep the dies sharp, I can see the defects in the parts punched out. I have come to appreciate sharp tools. Sharp tools are safe tools and work more efficiently.

God's word is flawless. If used daily it will act like a file to remove the imperfections in my life. As with the file, I need to use God's Word frequently for it to be effective. God's Word will keep me safe in a dangerous world and I too will run more efficiently in doing the work my Heavenly Father has for me.

Prayer

Dear Lord, I pray the Holy Spirit will reveal to me my imperfections. Let me not be resistant to the abrasiveness of God's Word as He sharpens my Christian witness. Amen.

JANUARY 28

DAY 28

But everything should be done in a fitting and orderly way.
1 CORINTHIANS 14:40

Storing the Tools

Within the first several weekends of working on the cabin, I accumulated most of the tools I needed each week to continue my work. To save time I kept all of my tools at the construction site. At the end of each workday, I laid all of the equipment on top of the picnic table. For protection from the moisture, I wiped the exposed areas of metal with an oily rag and put a tarp over them. I weighed the tarp down with four two-foot logs. By doing this, all of my tools were protected from the elements, in order, and readably available.

God is a God of order. I need not look any further than His creation to prove this point; everything has its place. God wants us to keep our lives orderly as well. According to the Psalmist, God is my hiding place in whom I can be protected me from life's trouble (Ps. 32:7).

Prayer

> *Thank You, Heavenly Father, for providing a place for me where I can go to be protected from life's corrosive effects, so that when I come out I will be ready for You to use. Amen.*

JANUARY 29
DAY 29

And with your feet fitted with the readiness that comes from the gospel of peace.
EPHESIANS 6:15

Comfortable Footwear

One thing is for certain: if your feet are not comfortable, your workday will not be very long. A big part of that is keeping your feet dry and warm. The year before the building of my cabin, I bought a pair of mukluks. They are thinsulated, lined, and waterproof boots. They slip on and come up just below my knee. They turned out to be the ideal footwear for working on my cabin during the snow-covered months of February and March.

God also has some special footwear for his children. My feet need to be fitted with the gospel of peace. Then I need to use them to fulfill the great commission (Matt. 28:16–20).

Prayer

> *Dear Heavenly Father, I pray that my feet will not grow weary in taking the gospel to those who have not heard it. Amen.*

JANUARY 30
DAY 30

Do not conform any longer to the pattern of this world, but be trans-
formed by the renewing of your mind. Then you will be able to test
and approve what God's will is—his good, pleasing and perfect will.

ROMANS 12:2

Building the Cabin in the Right Direction

When deciding where to build my cabin I also took into consideration the direction the cabin would be facing. I did not want my door
opening onto a tree or a large rock. When I stepped out from the cabin
door, I did not want to be stepping downhill. I also was concerned to
have the roof and chimney clear from any overhanging limbs.

God has a special direction in which He wants my life to go. He
wants me to keep my life free from worldly obstacles that would prevent
fellowship with Him. If I am obedient to God and strive to become
more Christlike, I can be confident that where I am at is where He
wants me to be.

Prayer

Dear Heavenly Father, I pray that I am going in the direction
in which You want me to be heading, and that my obedience
will be pleasing to You, for You to accomplish Your will for my
life. Amen.

JANUARY 31
DAY 31

The path of the righteous is level; O upright One,
you make the way of the righteous smooth.
ISAIAH 26:7

Cabin Path

I have two paths leading to the doorway of my cabin. One path comes in from the backside. I call this one my nature trail. In spring, summer, and fall, it passes through a carpet of ferns and you need to cross over two log walkways that take you over running spring water. The other path comes in from the front. This path is bordered with logs and is entered from my driveway. Both paths are kept clear of any obstacles. Any bumps, divots, or holes made by removing rocks were smoothed over to make the walking surface as level as possible.

Though the circumstances surrounding my life may be rough, I can be confident that if I am obedient to God's Word and walk according to His ways, He will make the path in my life smooth according to His promises.

Prayer

Dear Heavenly Father, help me to walk according to Your Word so I may avoid all of the world's stumbling blocks. Amen.

FEBRUARY 1
DAY 32

But encourage one another daily, as long as it is called Today,
so that none of you may be hardened by sin's deceitfulness.
HEBREWS 3:13

Frozen Ground

The ground was frozen and snow-covered. In other words, it was hard. My pick and digging iron came in handy at this point. By using them I was able to penetrate the hard ground. I removed rocks and leveled the area where my first logs were placed to form the corners of the cabin.

There are many people in the world today whose hearts are hardened to the love of God. The longer I resisted God and the good news He had for me the harder my heart became. Unfortunately, some people have grown so hard they cannot feel Jesus knocking at the door of their heart (Rev. 3:20). Even as a believer in Christ I need to be careful not to form habits that would harden areas of my heart, keeping me from being sensitive to God's prompting.

Prayer

Dear Heavenly Father, I pray that I will keep the soil of my heart easy to till so it is good for You to grow my spiritual fruit. Amen.

FEBRUARY 2
DAY 33

Now we see but a poor reflection as in a mirror; then
we shall see face to face. Now I know in part; then I
shall know fully, even as I am fully known.
1 CORINTHIANS 13:12

Clear Weekends

Most of the weekends when I worked on my cabin I was blessed with clear skies. If you went back and checked the National Weather Service records for the year 2005 in northeastern Pennsylvania, you would find the weather on weekends from February to September was at least ninety percent free of rain. Working with the sun out was a big plus. My tools didn't get wet, it kept me warm during the months of winter, and I stayed dry. The clear blue skies with puffy white clouds made my cabin-building experience a joyful one.

There is going to come a day when I see clearly what were once mysteries of the faith. That day will come when I go through the doorway from life to death and see Jesus fact to face. My heart will be filled with praise and joy for then I will know in full.

Prayer

Jesus, help me to keep my eyes focused on You, especially through the clouded times of trials and tribulations until the day we meet in glory. Amen.

FEBRUARY 3

DAY 34

Do your best to present yourself to God as one approved,
a workman who does not need to be ashamed and
who correctly handles the word of truth.
2 TIMOTHY 2:15

Handling Tools Correctly

Tools are used to accomplish and make easier the tasks we are doing. Tools are meant to be helpful, not harmful. When using tools I try to follow all the safety precautions for each tool I am using. "Use the right tool for the right job" is a saying I learned at a young age. In other words, do not try to pry a rock out with a shovel. You will end up bending the spade or breaking the handle. Use a digging iron.

I am God's vessel. I need to do my best to present myself to God to meet his approval. I have a tool that will help me do this if I use it every day and handle it correctly. That tool is God's Word, the Bible.

Prayer

Dear Heavenly Father, help me to put You first each day by reading Your Word, giving the Holy Spirit the opportunity to reveal Your truths to me so I will meet Your approval. Amen.

FEBRUARY 4
DAY 35

The first thing Andrew did was to find his brother Simon and tell him, "We have found the Messiah."
JOHN 1:41

Laying the First Logs

It was time to get started. I had never done anything like this in my life before. One of my favorite toys as a boy growing up was my Lincoln Log set, so how hard could it be to build a cabin? I started the chainsaw and I cut four two-foot logs that were placed at the corners of my ten foot by twelve-foot cabin. I was now ready and eager to put in place my first layer of logs. I looked forward to each coming weekend and the prospect of adding another layer of logs.

When I first accepted Jesus as my personal Savior, I was full of joy and anticipation. I knew I could not keep this good news to myself. I had to tell someone. The first people I told were my children and family. My heart knew God did not want me to keep this newfound joy to myself.

Prayer

Heavenly Father, help me to be faithful in sharing the good news to those whom You want me to tell. Amen.

FEBRUARY 5
DAY 36

For all have sinned and fall short of the glory of God.
ROMANS 3:23

Fallen Timber

One of the main reasons I bought our home was the acre stand of pines on the property. I love those red pines. When I built the cabin, I was determined to preserve the evergreens. With this in mind, seventy percent of the cabin is constructed from previously fallen timber. If fallen timber could talk, I imagine it would say, "Oh boy, I am going to be used, I thought I was just going to lay here and rot away."

Ever since Adam and Eve sinned, every person born has fallen into sin. That is the bad news. The good news is that Jesus redeemed me from the curse of sin. Through His shed blood on the cross, he has covered my transgressions. Through faith in Christ, though once fallen, God can now use me for His glory.

Prayer

Dear Heavenly Father, I am grateful to You for restoring the fallen condition of humanity through the sanctifying blood of Your Son Jesus. Amen.

FEBRUARY 6
DAY 37

The heart is deceitful above all things and beyond cure. Who can understand it?
JEREMIAH 17:9

Rotten Logs

Some of the fallen timber on the property was too rotten to use. In most cases by just looking at it, I could see that it was not suitable. Other times I had to cut through the log to reveal the extent of the deterioration inside. I definitely knew a log was beyond usefulness when I could push a spike through it with my hand.

Without God, the heart of a man is beyond repair. Due to man's sin nature, my heart is rotten to the core. I am grateful that my Heavenly Father is compassionate, merciful, and full of grace. Unlike those unusable logs, God can use and desires to use me for His glory. I could never commit so many sins that they could not all be covered by the blood of Jesus.

Prayer

Thank You, Heavenly Father for Your desire to have none perish but everyone to come to repentance (2 Pet. 3:9). Amen.

FEBRUARY 7
DAY 38

If a man cleanses himself...he will be an instrument for noble purposes, made holy, useful to the Master and prepared to do any good work.
1 TIMOTHY 2:21

Moving the Logs

Cutting the logs to the length I needed them was the easy part. Where the log lay after it was cut would do me no good in the construction of the cabin. The log had to be moved, notched out, and put into place before it became a part of the cabin.

Was the log still a log when it was just lying on the ground? Yes, but it was not part of the cabin. Am I a Christian when I receive Jesus as my Savior? Yes, however, God needs to move me to where I will be most useful to Him. He wants me to become part of the body of His church.

As a group, we can edify one another, worship together and witness to our community. He might even move me to Shunk, Pennsylvania.

Prayer

> *Dear Heavenly Father, let me not resist when You desire to move me where You want to use me. Amen.*

FEBRUARY 8
DAY 39

On that day, when all the nations of the earth are gathered against her, I will make Jerusalem an immovable rock for all the nations. All who try to move it will injure themselves.
ZECHARIAH 12:3

Frozen to the Ground

If time allowed, at the end of the day I would try to cut logs to the length I needed. I would then lay them next to the cabin. Doing this would give me a head start on adding another layer to the cabin the following weekend. The only problem was I needed to pry the logs from the frozen ground and from one another with a digging iron. Even though the logs were only there for a week, it would be difficult getting them loose from winter's grip.

There are times in life when I get stuck in the business and routines of life. I get into a comfort zone and I do not want to move out of it. Having my daily devotions and always putting God first will help me from getting stuck in bad habits.

Prayer

> *Dear Heavenly Father, I pray I will be easily moved by the promptings of the Holy Spirit. Amen.*

FEBRUARY 9

DAY 40

Blessed are you when people insult you, persecute you and falsely say all kinds of evil against you because of me.
MATTHEW 5:11

Dragging Logs Uphill

Fortunately for me, the site where I built the cabin and from where I had to drag the logs was mostly level. There were those occasions, however, when I would have to maneuver a cut log uphill. This of course just added to the difficulty of getting the log to the cabin site where it could be used.

God does not promise that my Christian walk will always be easy. God's Word says that people will say false things against me and persecute me for following Jesus. Even though there are times when my Christian walk will be difficult, I need to follow Jesus. It is during these times that I think of the verse in the song "I Have Decided to Follow Jesus": "Though no one joins me, I still will follow."

Prayer

Dear Heavenly Father, help me to continue to put one foot in front of the other even when the world is trying to hold me back from becoming more Christlike. Amen.

FEBRUARY 10

DAY 41

Therefore, since we are surrounded by such a great cloud of witnesses, let us throw off everything that hinders and the sin that so easily entangles, and let us run with perseverance the race marked out for us.
HEBREWS 12:1

One Step at a Time

I set goals for myself each weekend. In the beginning, it was to add another layer of logs to the cabin plus cut logs for the following weekend. This was the minimum I wanted to get done each week. I also had a monthly timetable for tasks to be completed, such as chinking, hanging the door, putting in the wood-burning stove and the roof. Concentrating only on the project ahead helped me not to be overwhelmed by the idea of building a cabin. One of my life mottos is this: doing a little consistently accomplishes great things.

That is how God wants me to walk with Him. I need to demonstrate perseverance in my Christian walk. I need to be consistent in my daily quiet time with my Heavenly Father. Each day I need to strive to be one more step closer in becoming more like Jesus.

Prayer

> *Dear Heavenly Father, help me to persevere in my walk with You especially during those times when I am in the valley of life. Amen.*

FEBRUARY 11
DAY 42

God saw all that he had made, and it was very good. And there was evening, and there was morning—the sixth day.
GENESIS 1:31

Seeing the Design

It was a good day when I got my first layer of logs in place. The back was first, then the two logs on the front side. I used two logs on the front because I came in from both sides and left the middle open for my door instead of using a full-length log and having to cut the door out later. After the front and back logs were in place, I notched out the side logs and spiked them in place. I made sure everything was square and level and then stopped for the day. I could actually see the design of the cabin taking shape. There was no stopping me now.

After God created the heavens and the earth and all that are in them, He was very pleased. One of the ways God reveals himself is through His creation. I truly enjoy the wonderful testimony of God's handiwork.

Prayer

Heavenly Father, help me to see You in the splendor and wonder of Your creation and not to be caught up in man's accomplishments. Amen.

FEBRUARY 12
DAY 43

Folly delights a man who lacks judgment, but a man of understanding keeps a straight course.
PROVERBS 15:21

Red Pines Grow Straight

Have I mentioned that I love the stand of pines on my property? For the next several days, I would like to discuss the attributes of the red pines which attract me to them. The first of which is how they grow perfectly straight. To me it is pleasing to the eyes to see the uniformity of a stand of pine trees. Every tree is close to being equal in diameter and height, with each growing straight towards the heavens.

Satan knows each of my weaknesses and is the master of twisting my life astray. I need to grow tall in the Spirit and keep my focus straight on the things of God.

Prayer

Dear Heavenly Father, help me to walk straight into Your arms, by avoiding branching off towards what the world has to offer for temporary fulfillment. Amen.

FEBRUARY 13
DAY 44

I tell you the truth, he who believes has everlasting life.
JOHN 6:47

Evergreen

Long after all the other trees have lost their foliage, the red pines remain green. The name evergreen covers all the conifers that remain green throughout all the seasons. In winter they are especially beautiful to see with a coating of fresh snow. The white snow on top of the green needles with a deep blue sky as a backdrop makes for a beautiful picture.

I can hardly imagine how glorious heaven is going to be. God promises that by my faith in His Son, Jesus Christ, I will have everlasting life with Him in heaven.

Prayer

Thank you, Heavenly Father, for the hope of living forever with You in the glory of my heavenly home. Amen.

FEBRUARY 14
DAY 45

May my meditation be pleasing to him, as I rejoice in the Lord.
PSALM 104:34

A Carpet of Pine Needles

Even though the pines remain green, each year they go through a cycle of new growth and a certain amount of the older pine needles turn brown and fall to the ground. On a windy fall day, the needles fall to the ground and cover the picnic table, benches, chairs, and forest floor. Besides having to clean off the camp furniture and raking them away from the fire ring, the needles fall harmlessly to the ground making a soft carpet that is pleasing to walk on.

Praise the Lord. How good it is to sing praises to our God, how pleasant and fitting to praise him (Ps. 147:1)! Our Heavenly Father wants us to live Godly lives so our walk is pleasing to Him.

Prayer

Dear Lord, it is my prayer to give you praise and walk with you in a way that will bless those around me. Amen.

FEBRUARY 15
Day 46

Now may the Lord of peace himself give you peace at all times and in every way. The Lord be with all of you.
2 THESSALONIANS 3:16

Soft Breeze Through the Pines

The rhythmic crashing of ocean waves on a beach has a calming affect on me. I get a similar feeling when I hear the softest of breezes blowing through the tops of the pines. I enjoy lying in my hammock on a warm spring day, cool summer day, or a breezy fall day when the sky is deep blue and there are puffy cumulus clouds in the sky. For me it does not get any more peaceful or relaxing than to just lay there and watch the clouds pass over while listening to the crescendo of the wind passing through pines.

Even in the most hectic circumstances I face in life, I can experience the peace of God. Knowing that God is in control, and He loves me and comforts me through the most difficult of times.

Prayer

Thank You, Heavenly Father, for the peace I have even when everything around me seems chaotic. Amen.

FEBRUARY 16
DAY 47

Take my yoke upon you and learn from me, for I am gentle
and humble in heart, and you will find rest for your souls.
MATTHEW 11:29

Always Cooler

There is a lot of shade in the pines. The canopy the red pines form
and the motion of the branches from the slightest breeze prevents any
concentrated warming effect the suns rays might have had on the forest
floor. There is also a run of spring water that flows through the pines.
In midsummer the water temperature does not rise above sixty degrees.
Between the filtered sunlight and cool spring water, it is usually ten
degrees cooler in the pines. This makes for a good refuge where I can
rest comfortably from the heat of summer and regain my strength.

I am a pilgrim in this world. As a Christian, I need a place to go for
protection and rest. God is our refuge and strength (Ps. 46:1) and if we
turn to Him, he will give rest to our soul.

Prayer

Dear Heavenly Father, I pray that I will find daily refreshment
in Your Word so my witness for You will bring rejuvenation to
those in the world. Amen.

FEBRUARY 17
DAY 48

And live a life of love, just as Christ loved us and gave himself
up for us as a fragrant offering and sacrifice to God.
EPHESIANS 5:2

Pine Scent

One of the memories I enjoy most of Christmas is the bringing home of the Christmas tree and the way the house is filled with the scent of pine. In my stand of pines, I can enjoy this fragrance on a more regular basis. If the pine scent in the air is not detectable to my sense of smell, there are times when I will break some pine needles in my hand to release the pine oils just so I can enjoy the fresh scent of pine.

God wants my daily walk with Him to be a sweet fragrance to those around me. I need to live my life in such a way that those I meet will be attracted to the love I have through Christ.

Prayer

Heavenly Father, I pray my witness will be an attractive fragrance to those in the world, giving me an opportunity to share the love You have for them through Your Son, Jesus Christ. Amen.

FEBRUARY 18
DAY 49

Finally, be strong in the Lord and in his mighty power.
EPHESIANS 6:10

Tall and Strong

I built my cabin in 2006. According to my neighbor, it was his grandfather who planted the red pines back in the 1930s. That is seventy-plus years since his grandfather planted those trees. They have withstood blizzards, ice storms, sleet, high winds, torrential rains, hailstorms, and drought. Despite the hardships nature has brought upon them, they remain a healthy stand of red pines. They are tall and strong. They average two feet in diameter and forty feet in height.

No matter what tribulation I face in my Christian walk, I need to remain strong in the Lord. It is Satan's desire to break my relationship with God. He wants to render me useless for the work my Heavenly Father has for me.

Prayer

> *Dear Heavenly Father, help me to withstand the test of time by remaining strong in the Lord. Amen.*

FEBRUARY 19
DAY 50

He is like a tree planted by streams of water, which yields its fruit in season and whose leaf does not wither. Whatever he does prospers.
PSALM 1:3

Well Rooted

Over the years, the decomposition of fallen pine needles, bark, limbs, and other woodland debris has made a rich black acidic soil for the roots of the pines to prosper in. The springs that run underground provide moisture and minerals even during summer's driest conditions. The roots are intertwined with one another and run deep through the crevices of the mountain stone-laden landscape. This provides secure support for the forty feet of growth above ground, capable of withstanding strong blustery weather.

My faith needs to be deeply rooted in the truths of God's work to stand up against the winds of false philosophies preached by the world. I want to live my life so that I will experience the living water Jesus has to offer.

Prayer

> *Heavenly Father, I pray that the taproots of my spiritual life will be well-watered with the truth of Your Word to keep me from wavering in a world of relativism. Amen.*

FEBRUARY 20
DAY 51

Blessed are the pure in heart, for they will see God.
MATTHEW 5:8

Seeing Clearly

I like the stand of red pines because you can see from one side to the other. The reason for this is two-fold. First, there is no underbrush to block my view, and secondly, as the red pine grows the lower branches die and eventually fall off. Therefore, from the forest floor to ten feet up the trunk of each tree, there is no growth to obstruct my view.

It is my desire as a Christian to see God clearly. Not visibly as I will when I get to heaven but to see Him by understanding His will and the promptings of the Holy Spirit. To obtain this intimate relationship I need to break off sinful habits. By being obedient to God's statues, my fellowship with Him will be unobstructed.

Prayer

Heavenly Father, help me to remove the dark areas of sin from my heart so I can see You clearly through the eyes of the Holy Spirit. Amen.

FEBRUARY 21
DAY 52

For the wages of sin is death, but the gift of God is eternal life in Christ Jesus our Lord.
ROMANS 6:23

A Tree Had to Die

I used many trees that were already dead and on the ground. I cut sections of logs out of these fallen trees first and made brush piles out of the tops. It helped to clean up the property while making cover for the smaller animals in the woods at the same time. As much as I did not want to, I had to cut down four red pines and two hemlocks to finish the cabin. Those trees had to die in order to be useful to me in completing the cabin.

Jesus had to die for God to complete His plan of restoring mankind to Himself. Jesus died to pay the wages of sin. God valued my life so much that He allowed His Son to give His life for me.

Prayer

Dear Heavenly Father, help me never to forget what my sins cost You. Help me to walk obediently with you all the days of my life. Amen.

FEBRUARY 22
DAY 53

Sitting down, Jesus called the Twelve and said, "If anyone wants to be first, he must be the very last, and the servant of all."
MARK 9:35

Fallen Pine Needles

If you live in an area where you have to rake leaves or pine needles during the fall of the year, I am sure this thought has crossed your mind: Why are we not knee deep in leaves when we take a walk in the woods? Yet from year to year, there does not seem to be any more leaves in the woods than from the year before. In God's wonderful cycle of creation, the dead organic matter decomposes to provide the new growth of spring with essential minerals. I take advantage of this process by using the fallen pine needles as mulch around my azaleas and rhododendron. So what seems useless is actually used for good.

Satan is the master of making Christians feel unworthy of doing God's work. There are times when I feel I would be the last person God would use to accomplish His plans. The truth is God can and will use me despite my shortcomings.

Prayer

Heavenly Father, use my fallen condition for Your glory as I continue to become more Christlike each day. Amen.

FEBRUARY 23
DAY 54

Blessed is the man who perseveres under trial, because when he has stood the test, he will receive the crown of life that God has promised to those who love him.
JAMES 1:12

Ferns

For the past eleven days, I have discussed a variety of attributes that I enjoy about the acre stand of red pine on my property. I have already mentioned the lack of undergrowth, which allows me to see clearly through the pines. The only plant that does thrive in this ecosystem is ferns. I love the fern plants. They line my path going up to the cabin, grow by the springs, and hang over the log walkways crossing over the running water. The fern is the predominate plant that takes hold in these adverse conditions. You definitely would not want to plant a garden in this soil that is covered in pine needles and laden with mountain rocks.

I face different degrees of adversity each day. It is God's desire for me to grow more Christlike through the trials I face. I need to persevere under trials. Perseverance develops maturity and adds to my testimony.

Prayer

Dear Heavenly Father, help me to flourish as I pass through the trials of life so I may be able to encourage others facing similar circumstances. Amen.

FEBRUARY 24
DAY 55

*Being confident of this, that he who began a good work in you
will carry it on to completion until the day of Christ Jesus.*
PHILIPPIANS 1:6

Notching the Logs

The old adage "practice makes perfect" was never truer than when it came to the technique for notching out the logs. I did have some idea of how to perform this task from books I had read and from playing with Lincoln Logs. I soon found that I was limited on which notch to use by the tools I had. By the third layer of logs, I had perfected an efficient and effective technique for notching my logs.

My Christian walk is a work in progress. I was not perfect when I received Jesus as my Savior nor will I ever be perfect in my carnal body. However, if I am faithful in going to church, praying, performing daily devotions, and reading the Bible, God promises to finish the work He has begun in my life.

Prayer

*Heavenly Father, I pray that my practice of devoting my life to
You will provide You with an improved vessel to work with.
Amen.*

FEBRUARY 25
DAY 56

*On the contrary, we speak as men approved by God
to be entrusted with the gospel. We are not trying
to please men but God, who tests our hearts.*
1 THESSALONIANS 2:4

First Attempt

On my first attempt, I tried to make the notches in the log square. When I put the square notched-out log on the un-notched log below it, I noticed big gaps on the side of the notch. A square notch on a round log was not a good fit. I would have to notch the log below also for the square notch to work but that was twice the work. Also making a square notch with the tools I had was challenging. I did not have a good chisel to clean up the notch properly. I had to try something else.

I do not always get it right the first time in my Christian walk either. Often times I try to please God by doing things my way instead of letting the Holy Spirit guide my actions.

Prayer

> *Dear Heavenly Father, help me to be sensitive to the prompt-ings of Your Holy Spirit so that my witness for You will be as You desire. Amen.*

FEBRUARY 26
DAY 57

Then Jesus declared, "I am the bread of life. He who comes to me will never go hungry, and he who believes in me will never be thirsty."
JOHN 6:35

Second Attempt

I laid the log I wanted to notch on top of logs where it needed to fit in place. I determined the width of my notch by the thickness of the log it was laying on. After marking the width, I would take my chainsaw and make nine cuts. I used the chainsaw bar to measure the depth of my cut. In the middle of the notch, I cut down the full width of the chain bar then on each side I would make four cuts two inches apart with each cut being an inch deeper than the previous cut. When done it reminded me of a loaf of bread. I took my ax and knocked each slice of wood out leaving me with a semi-circle notch that fit perfectly on the log it was laying on.

Each notch reminded me of Jesus saying, "I am the bread of life." I need to be living in the spirit and not the flesh. If I eat the bread of life and seek first the kingdom of God, all of my physical needs will be met (Matt. 6:31–34).

Prayer

> *Help me, Heavenly Father, to be more concerned about nourishing myself with the spiritual bread of life that Jesus has to offer than with the physical food You promise to provide. Amen.*

FEBRUARY 27
DAY 58

When you were dead in your sins and in the uncircumcision of your sinful nature, God made you alive with Christ. He forgave us all our sins, having canceled the written code, with its regulations, that was against us and that stood opposed to us; he took it away, nailing it to the cross.
COLOSSIANS 2:13–14

Eight-Inch Spikes

For each layer of logs I would have to make four notches. One log for the back wall and one log for the front wall. Then I would repeat the process for the two side walls. After having two logs notched out I would set them in place. I would then check and double check for squareness by stretching a string diagonally from corner to corner and making sure the measurements were equal. When this was done, I would then hammer an eight-inch spike into each corner. I needed to use a mallet to pound each spike through the log and into the log it was laying on.

I could not help but think of the crucifixion of my Lord and Savior Jesus Christ every time I performed this task. The images of the Roman soldiers pounding the spikes through the hands and feet of Jesus onto the cross would pass through my mind.

Prayer

Heavenly Father, help me to remember the sacrifice Jesus made for my sins each day to help me from driving any more nails into His hands and feet. Amen.

FEBRUARY 28
DAY 59

For the wages of sin is death, but the gift of God is eternal life in Christ Jesus our Lord.
ROMANS 6:23

Twenty-Five Cents

I needed four spikes per layer. At twenty-five cents per spike, each layer cost a total of one dollar. My cabin is eight layers high; besides the one gallon of fuel it cost to run the chainsaw, my monetary investment building four cabin walls was merely eight dollars.

Even more amazing is what it cost me to have my relationship restored with my Heavenly Father and my sins forgiven. It was free! God paid the debt of sin for me; the gift of God is eternal life through Jesus Christ. All I owe is acknowledgement of Jesus as my personal Savior. The blood of Jesus and the grace of God have paid for my atonement.

Prayer

Heavenly Father, I pray that my gratitude will be evident through my obedience to You for paying a debt I was incapable of paying. Amen.

MARCH 1
DAY 60

*If you have any encouragement from being united with
Christ…then make my joy complete by being like-minded,
having the same love, being one in spirit and purpose.*
PHILIPPIANS 2:1–2

Joining One Log to Another

After notching out the logs, I would roll them over so the notch
would fit onto the log below it. Then I would tap them until my corners
were square and plumb. With the logs being frozen and covered with
a dusting of snow, they would slide very easy. When in place, I would
use one ten-penny nail on each side to keep the log in place while I
pounded the eight-inch spike through the notched log into the log
below it. When done, the logs were securely joined to the log below. I
would then remove the two ten-penny nails.

We are securely joined with our Lord and Savior Jesus. There is
nothing that can separate me from the love of God (Rom. 8:37–39).

Prayer

*Dear Heavenly Father, help me to remember daily the union I
have with Christ. Enable me to share the same unconditional
love You have for me with those I encounter each day. Amen.*

MARCH 2
DAY 61

*Therefore, go make disciples of all nations, baptizing them in
the name of the Father and of the Son and of the Holy Spirit.*
MATTHEW 28:19

Many Logs Become One

After six weekends, the four walls of the cabin were complete. The
thirty-two logs making up the four walls were in place with each layer
being square, plumb, and securely in place with the layer below it. Six
and a half weeks ago, those thirty-two logs were lying on the ground

or growing in close proximity to the construction site. Now united together the logs formed the four walls of one log cabin.

God is three persons in one. He is God, our Heavenly Father who has reconciled Himself to mankind; He is God, who became flesh in the person of Jesus Christ; and He is God the Holy Spirit who fills the heart of every believer.

Prayer

Thank you, Heavenly Father, for revealing yourself through Your Son Jesus Christ. Thank you for His sacrifice for my sins. Thank you for Your Counselor the Holy Spirit who dwells within me. Amen.

MARCH 3
DAY 62

Therefore, my dear friends, as you have always obeyed— not only in my presence, but how much more in my absence—continue to work out your salvation.
PHILIPPIANS 2:12

Another Layer of Logs Complete

I started each weekend by picking out the tools I needed and choosing the logs to be used for another layer. Then it was lifting, pushing, sawing, chopping, measuring, and pounding. At the end of the day, I would put my tools away and look at the cabin to inspect the layer of logs just completed. The walls would be one log higher. It was then I felt the satisfaction of a good day's work and felt motivated to continue the following week.

There are times in my Christian walk when I do not feel very Christ-like. Even during these periods, I need to maintain my walk with Christ and be the servant He wants me to be to others. As I bring joy into the lives of others, it brings back the joy in my heart and gives me the motivation to continue striving to become more like Christ each day.

Prayer

Dear Heavenly Father, remind me to look back on answered prayers and my Christian testimony to give me the inspiration to continue my walk through the world. Amen.

MARCH 4

DAY 63

You hypocrite, first take the plank out of your own eye, and then you will see clearly to remove the speck from your brother's eye.
MATTHEW 7:5

Flying Chips of Wood

After I used my chainsaw to make the cuts I needed for the notch, it was time to put my ax to use. I always made sure I had my safety glasses on for this job. Wood chips would be flying in every direction. I started in from one side of the notch then on the other side. At first large chunks of wood were cut from the notch as the ax blade did its job. Then as I chipped the notch into shape, smaller splinters of wood would become airborne. I needed to be careful not to get these pieces into my eye.

When I witness to others, I have to be sensitive to where I was before accepting Jesus as my personal Savior. I cannot let the splinters of sin that were forgiven me, keep me from forgiving others.

Prayer

Dear Lord, remove any obstructions in my eyes so that I may see our Heavenly Father more clearly. Amen.

MARCH 5
DAY 64

*Let us fix our eyes on Jesus, the author and perfecter of our faith,
who for the joy set before him endured the cross, scorning its
shame, and sat down at the right hand of the throne of God.*
HEBREWS 12:2

Hit the Spike

Pounding the eight-inch spikes in place was one of the more satisfying jobs while building the cabin. It meant another log was in place and the cabin was another log higher. Even though the spikes were three-eighths of an inch thick, if I did not hit them squarely they would bend. Therefore, I took extra precautions to hit the nail on the head. I can remember bending one spike that was already half of the way in and I needed a crowbar to get it back out.

Each day I need to keep my eyes fixed on Jesus. By doing this it will keep me from falling into a sinful habit. The deeper I let the roots of sin grow in my heart the harder it is to break free from its bondage.

Prayer

*Heavenly Father, help me to hit Your spiritual mark each day
so that I will be a blessing to You and to those I encounter.
Amen.*

MARCH 6
DAY 65

*People who want to get rich fall into temptation and
a trap and into many foolish and harmful desires
that plunge men into ruin and destruction.*
1 TIMOTHY 6:9

Do Not Cut too Deep

The bar on the chainsaw measured six inches. Most of the logs that I used were twelve inches or more in diameter. Therefore, when I made my middle cut for the notch I would only go as deep as the width of my chain and chain bar. This way I knew I was not cutting too deep. I was very careful not to cut too deep or the log would be ruined.

The Bible warns me not to fall into the trap of obtaining material wealth. It can lead to many foolish decisions and harmful desires which if carried out would ruin my fellowship with my Heavenly Father. I need to remember the love of money is a root of all kinds of evil (1 Tim. 6:10).

Prayer

Dear Heavenly Father, help me not to fall too deep into temptations where they become a habit and ruin my fellowship with You. Amen.

MARCH 7

DAY 66

Watch and pray so that you will not fall into temptation. The spirit is willing, but the body is weak.
MATTHEW 26:41

After a Long Day

I would try to get started by eight a.m. each day I worked on the cabin. I usually took a lunch break at noon. My lunch breaks varied anywhere from eating an apple on the run to heading up to the house for a meal prepared by my wife. I would be back in my full construction stride by one p.m. By five p.m. I would be stopping for the day. Even though there were still several hours of daylight left, by five o'clock my body had usually had enough after nine hours of chain sawing, ax swinging, and log lifting. My mind was willing but my body said stop.

I think my adversary likes to attack especially when I am trying to pray or read God's Word. My spirit is willing but many times I find my mind wandering or my eyes getting heavy with sleep.

Prayer

> *Heavenly Father, help me to stay focused and alert during times of worship and quiet times with You. Amen.*

MARCH 8

DAY 67

I will make justice the measuring line and righteousness the plumb line.
ISAIAH 28:17

Keep It Square and Plumb

With each passing weekend, another layer of logs was completed. With each layer, I was careful to make sure that the corners were square and the walls were plumb. To check for squareness I used a string that was premeasured from the very first layer. I stretched it from corner to corner diagonally until the markings on the string were the same as the first layer. I tied an eight-penny nail to a string to check whether the walls were plumb.

Jesus said, "If you love me you will obey me" (John 14:15). God desires for my life to be plumb with the ordinances he has given me to live by. By being obedient to God's Word and by not quenching the Holy Spirit, I will remain true to the plan God has for my life.

Prayer

> *Dear Heavenly Father, help me to measure up to Your expectations so that Your plumb line of righteousness will keep me squared away for the plan You have for my life. Amen.*

MARCH 9
DAY 68

*But seek first his kingdom and his righteousness, and
all these things will be given to you as well.*
MATTHEW 6:33

Keep it Level

All my corners were square and all four walls were plumb. I still had
one more measurement I needed to keep a close eye on. The four walls
needed to be level to one another in height. Since my logs were not
exactly the same diameter, I had to place thicker and thinner logs from
side to side and front to back to maintain the same height. Of course it
was the last layer that was crucial. My crossbeams had to be perfectly
straight or my roof would have been lopsided.

In life, I need to keep my priorities straight. The gospel of Matthew
tells me to seek first the kingdom of God. If I put God first in my life,
everything else will fall right into place.

Prayer

*Heavenly Father, I pray to be level-minded by always putting
You first in my daily activities. Amen.*

MARCH 10
DAY 69

Hide your face from my sins and blot out all my iniquity.
PSALM 51:9

Misplaced Tools

On several occasions, I can remember having to look for a tool
I needed to use. In most of the cases, the tool missing was the ax,
hammer, or mallet, the three tools I interchanged most frequently. I

had a one-foot log facing up in the middle of the cabin that I used for a table on which to place tools when not in use. Therefore, when I would go for a tool and it was not there, the search was on. It is amazing how well camouflaged an old brown-handled hammer can be lying in pine needles and wood chips. It was hidden from my sight.

Sometimes I lose sight of God in my daily walk and sin against Him. God hides His face from my sin and prevents me from enjoying the fellowship He desires. I need to find my way back to my Heavenly Father by repenting for my sin and asking for forgiveness.

Prayer

>*Help me, Heavenly Father, to keep my eyes focused on You so that I will not lose sight of the plans You have for me. Amen.*

MARCH 11
DAY 70

Suppose one of you has a hundred sheep and loses one of them. Does he not leave the ninety-nine in the open country and go after the lost sheep until he finds it?
LUKE 15:4

Finding Misplaced Tools

Usually when I misplaced a tool, I would have it back in my hands within a minute. I can only remember one time when it took me the better part of an hour to find my hammer. Whether it took me a minute or an hour to find my tool, two things were always true. One, everything stopped until I found the missing tool and second, the happiness I felt in locating the tool.

Jesus would have died for one lost sinner. Jesus tells the parable of a shepherd who left his ninety-nine sheep to go look for his one lost sheep. When one sinner repents, the heavens rejoice (Luke 15:7).

Prayer

Thank You, dear Heavenly Father, for loving me so much that You would have sent Your Son just for me. Amen.

MARCH 12
DAY 71

No one can serve two masters. Either he will hate the one and love the other, or he will be devoted to the one and despise the other. You cannot serve both God and Money.
MATTHEW 6:24

Straddling the Log

For the first four layers of logs, I could either stoop or stand while pounding the spikes in. When I got to the fifth layer, the height was too high for me to swing the mallet with the strength and accuracy I needed to drive the spike. I had to straddle the log horseback style to get the job accomplished.

This does not work with God. As a Christian, I cannot straddle the fence. I will not be an effective tool for God's use if I live like the world Monday through Saturday and worship God on Sunday. I cannot serve two masters.

Prayer

Heavenly Father, help me to live in the Spirit and not in my flesh, so that my life will be a valued tool to be used for Your glory. Amen.

MARCH 13
DAY 72

Be still, and know that I am God; I will be exalted
among the nations, I will be exalted in the earth.
PSALM 46:10

When the Sawing and Pounding Stops

Being outside was one of the best parts of working on the cabin each weekend, especially when I was not making noise by the pounding on nails or cutting through logs with my chainsaw. When everything was quiet and still, I would find myself listening to the sounds of nature. The cry of a hawk high above, a crow cawing in the distance, a tom gobbling in early spring, or the chorus of songbirds high in the pines were just some of the sounds heard in moments of quietness.

With all the responsibilities I have in my daily life, my days are filled with activity. I need to set a time each day when I will stop what I am doing and be still, quiet my heart and mind, and listen for the promptings of the Holy Spirit. I need to tune in to the voice of God.

Prayer

> *Dear Heavenly Father, I pray that as I take time to be still*
> *and listen, my heart will be in tune to the sound of Your voice.*
> *Amen.*

MARCH 14
DAY 73

Wise men store up knowledge, but the mouth of a fool invites ruin.
PROVERBS 10:14

Soaks Up Water Like a Sponge

The ground at the site where I built the cabin is very porous. It soaks up water like a sponge. The soil is rich black humus with a layer of pine needles on top. Under this thin layer of dirt is a seemingly endless supply of mountain stone. Somehow, this is an ideal ecosystem for pines and ferns to grow. Usually no matter how much rain or melting snow we have, the ground soaks it up.

God has given me His Word, the Bible. I need to soak up God's work like a sponge. It is very important for me to read God's instruction manual on a daily basis and to hide His Word in my hearts.

Prayer

Heavenly Father, as I read your Word daily, reveal Your truths to me so I can live a pure and holy life. Amen.

MARCH 15
DAY 74

You prepare a table before me in the presence of my enemies. You anoint my head with oil; my cup overflows. Surely, goodness and love will follow me all the days of my life, and I will dwell in the house of the LORD forever.
PSALM 23:5–6

Overflowing

I could count on one hand the number of times we got enough rain for the ground to become saturated. When this happens the soil is so full of water it overflows, forming pools of water in low spots. After a day without rain, the pools of water return below ground level.

I am grateful that God's blessings are not so few nor gone in a day. Truthfully, my life is overflowing with the blessings of God. Those days when I am having a pity party for myself, all I need to do is count my blessings one by one. Inevitably, I begin to feel better before I run out of things with which God has blessed me.

Prayer

> *Thank You, Heavenly Father, for each breath You give me. Help me to be grateful and content with all Your blessings in my life. Amen.*

MARCH 16
DAY 75

As the deer pants for streams of water, so my soul pants for you, O God. My soul thirsts for God, for the living God. When can I go and meet with God?
PSALM 42:1–2

Streams of Spring Water

When the ground was excavated for the house we live in, a spring-fed pond was included. There is one main stream of spring water running through the pines. The one trail leading to the cabin crosses over two other feeder springs that flow into the main stream of spring water.

Spring water has many attributes that I will highlight in the following days. For starters, though, the babbling streams of clear pure water are a constant reminder of how my soul should thirst for God. Spring water quenches my thirst like no other beverage. Likewise, there is only one God who can quench my longing for the meaning of life.

Prayer

> *Dear Heavenly Father, make it my habit to turn to You when I need to be refreshed from living in a spiritually parched world. Amen.*

MARCH 17
DAY 76

Whoever believes in me, as the Scripture has said,
streams of living water will flow from within him.
JOHN 7:38

Living Water

Water and life are almost synonymous. Water is life. Without water everything would die. All animal and plant life is dependent on water, from the aquatic animals that use water as a medium to live in to the terrestrial animals and plants that use water to maintain their physiological functions. If the rain stopped falling and streams stopped flowing, life as we know it would end. From the one-celled amoeba to mankind, we all need water to live.

Without Jesus, I am spiritually dead. I need Jesus to have eternal life. Without Jesus, I am separated from God. Jesus claimed victory over death through His resurrection (1 Cor. 15:54). The Gospel of John tells me that if I believe in Jesus, streams of living water will flow through me.

Prayer

Dear Lord, I hope the streams of living water flowing through me will quench the thirst of those in need of Your life-giving water. Amen.

MARCH 18
DAY 77

And we, who with unveiled faces all reflect the Lord's glory,
are being transformed into his likeness with ever-increasing
glory, which comes from the Lord, who is the Spirit.
2 CORINTHIANS 3:18

Seeing My Reflection

We have two spring-fed ponds that can be seen from our house. One is located in front of the house while the other is in the back. The pond in the front is much larger than the pond in the back. What is true of both is that on perfectly calm days when there are no ripples you can see a perfect image on the water of what is on the far side of the pond.

As I live my Christian life, I need to become more and more Christ-like with each passing day. It is my goal for the world to see a reflection of Jesus Christ in the way I live my daily life.

Prayer

Dear Heavenly Father, help me in whatever I do to do it in a way that reflects the perfect love of Jesus. Amen.

MARCH 19
DAY 78

Everyone who has this hope in him purifies himself, just as he is pure.
1 JOHN 3:3

Pure Enough to Drink

I enjoy landscaping our property but I do not look forward to planting trees. Because I know I will be hitting rock after one shovel full of dirt. However, the rocks I despise when planting act as a perfect filtration system for the spring water to run through. As the spring water percolates its way through the underground maze of rocks, impurities are removed from the water. Therefore, when the water breaks through the surface of the ground, you have water pure enough to drink.

God loves me so much that He sent His only Son to die on the cross to pay the debt for the penalty of sin. Sin is what separates me from God. There is no sin in heaven; our God is a pure God. I need the blood of Jesus to cover my sins for me to have the ability to fellowship with my Heavenly Father.

Prayer

> *Dear Heavenly Father, I am grateful that the purifying blood of Your Son Jesus Christ has removed the impurities of my sinful nature. Amen.*

MARCH 20
DAY 79

Worship the Lord with gladness; come before him with joyful songs.
PSALM 100:2

Babbling Brook

I enjoy writing songs. I wrote one song with the title "Easy to Love." The first line in the song says "It's easy to love little puppy dogs, babbling brooks, and your grandma's homemade sweet cherry pie." One of my favorite sounds in nature has to be the sound of rushing water over rocks and boulders. It is the sound of God's creation in action, like the rhythmic crashing of waves on the beach.

Similarly, God enjoys the joyful noise made by His bride the church. Encouraging words, praises to His name, and prayers are a few examples of sounds pleasing to God's ear. I am sure He also enjoys the sound of believers witnessing to a lost world.

Prayer

> *Heavenly Father, let my prayers, conversation, praises, and thanksgiving be a joyful noise to You. Amen.*

MARCH 21
DAY 80

The world and its desires pass away, but the man who does the will of God lives forever.
1 JOHN 2:17

Damp, Dreary, and Drizzly

I did not have blue skies and sunshine every weekend I worked on the cabin. There were only a few weekends during which the rain was steady enough to cancel work. But there were others that were damp, dreary, and drizzly. Not enough rain to cancel work but enough to make working conditions unpleasant.

Every day in my Christian walk is a mountaintop experience of worship and joy. My physical body gets tired and sometimes I get sick. I face the daily routine of meeting the daily needs of my body such as sleep and food. Many of us have schedules to keep. There are those who get up and go to school and others who work or take care of children and the household. As a Christian I am no longer of the world but live in the world (John 15:19).

Prayer

Heavenly Father, as I struggle with the physical and emotional difficulties of life, help me to live my life in the world in such a way that all I do will be pleasing to You. Amen.

MARCH 22
DAY 81

Yet the LORD longs to be gracious to you; he rises to show you compassion. For the LORD is a God of justice. Blessed are all who wait for him.
ISAIAH 30:18

Not Able to Work

From the second weekend of February 2005 to the second weekend of October 2005, you would have been able to find me out in the pines working on the cabin. There were only a handful of weekends when I was not able to work. The only two reasons for not working were rain and prior commitments made to church, family, or friends. When this would happen, I would just have to wait until the following weekend to continue work.

In our busy world of hurry up, I believe the patience of people to wait for something to be done is getting shorter. God answers prayer in three ways: yes, no, and wait. There are times when I need to wait on God's timing for the direction He desires me to go in my life.

Prayer

Dear Heavenly Father, help me to be patient during those times when I want to go but You say wait. Amen.

MARCH 23
DAY 82

Jesus answered, "Everyone who drinks this water will be thirsty again, but whoever drinks the water I give him will never thirst. Indeed, the water I give him will become in him a spring of water welling up to eternal life."
JOHN 4:13–14

Forever Flowing

The summer of 2000 was my family's first summer in Sullivan County. It was also one of the worst droughts for quite some time. Our county and the surrounding counties even had restrictions on water usage. The spring beside the cabin, however, never stopped flowing. Even during the dead of winter when the ground and ponds are frozen solid, the spring continues to flow. It provides water for all those animals that forage during the winter months. The stream of spring water is forever flowing.

I am glad that through Christ I have the hope of eternal life with God in heaven, where there will be no sin and I will be in the presence of the glory of God forever.

Prayer

Thank You, Heavenly Father, for the eternal life You have promised me through Your Son Jesus Christ. Amen.

MARCH 24
Day 83

*And do you worry about clothes? See how the lilies of the field
grow. They do not labor or spin. Yet I tell you that not even
Solomon in all his splendor was dressed like one of these.*
MATTHEW 6:28–29

Native Trout

Our driveway crosses over the stream of spring water. It flows through
a twenty-four inch sluice pipe covered with rocks and a mixture of small
stones and dirt making the surface of the driveway. When I walk the
dogs, I cross over the sluice pipe. Out of habit, I always look into the
pool of water formed by the water flowing out of the pipe. I could not
believe my eyes the day I saw native brook trout darting back and forth
in the water. The markings on a native brook trout are beautiful. They
are much brighter and more distinct than the stocked trout that fill our
streams during trout season.

You cannot outdo God when it comes to creation. It is impossible
to beat nature and its natural beauty. Man has tried through hybrids to
make the original better.

Prayer

> *Thank You, Heavenly Father, for revealing Yourself through
> the complexity and order of creation. Amen.*

MARCH 25
Day 84

*For our struggle is not against flesh and blood, but against the
rulers, against the authorities, against the powers of this dark world
and against the spiritual forces of evil in the heavenly realms.*
EPHESIANS 6:12

Anxious Moments

If you were to ask me at what times did I feel the most apprehensive, anxious, fearful, or nervous, I would answer you without hesitation. It was without a doubt when I had to cut down a tree. I do not like cutting down trees. First, I just don't like cutting down a mature tree—I would rather look at it—and secondly, too many things can go wrong. I used all the safety measures I knew when bringing down a mature red pine.

I need to walk carefully in the world I live in. I live in a spiritually dangerous world. Satan knows my weaknesses and is a master at causing me to stumble in my walk with the Lord. If I take precautions to keep my eyes on the Lord and live in the spirit and not the flesh, I will be able to live safely in a dangerous world.

Prayer

> *Dear Heavenly Father, help me not to quench the Holy Spirit*
> *as He attempts to lead me through each day. Amen.*

MARCH 26
DAY 85

All of this I have spoken while still with you. But the Counselor, the
Holy Spirit, whom the Father will send in my name, will teach you
all things and will remind you of everything I have said to you.
JOHN 14:25–26

Hung Up

After selecting the pine or hemlock to be cut down, I tried my best to cut it so it would fall all the way to the ground. Most times the room for error was not very big, which did not help the fact that I am a novice at cutting down trees. The inevitable would usually happen. As the tree would begin to come down, it would get hung up in the branches of another pine. When this occurred, it left me with the unpleasant task of getting it down the rest of the way.

I remember when I first became a Christian how intimidating the Bible was to me. I continually was hung up on what I was reading or how it applied to my life. Knowing this, God sent me a Helper. The Holy Spirit helps me to understand the truths of God and how they apply to my life.

Prayer

> *Dear Heavenly Father, help me to read Your Word through the eyes of the Holy Spirit so I will understand the truths You desire for me to know. Amen.*

MARCH 27
DAY 86

Guide me in your truth and teach me, for you are God my Savior, and my hope is in you all day long.
PSALM 25:5

Notching the Tree

I tried my best to cut the trees in such a way that when they fell, they would fall completely to the ground. I started by cutting out a notch one foot from the bottom on one side of the tree in the direction I wanted it to fall. Then on the backside of the notch I would make a straight cut just above the bottom of the notch until the tree began to fall. On several occasions, I was pleasantly surprised to find the tree falling in the direction I had planned.

From the day I was born, I have had people trying to guide my life. From parents and guidance counselors to pastors, relatives, my wife, and my friends, there will always be people in my life to help guide me through the decisions of life. Ultimately, it is my Heavenly Father who guides me in truth. He knows the plan He has for me that only I can accomplish.

Prayer

> *Heavenly Father, through Your Word, through prayer, and through my fellow Christians, guide me so that Your plan for me will fall in the direction You want me to go. Amen.*

MARCH 28
DAY 87

He who dwells in the shelter of the Most High will rest in the shadow of the Almighty. I will say of the LORD, "He is my refuge and my fortress, my God, in whom I trust."
PSALM 91:1–2

Brush Piles

The red pine is ideal for cabin building. The pines I cut down were thirty to forty feet tall. As they grow, the bottom branches die off leaving only the top ten feet with branches. I usually got two twelve-foot or three ten-foot logs out of each pine. I made brush piles out of the branches. The brush piles provide shelter and protection for the smaller residents on our property.

If I am obedient to God and receive His Son as my personal Savior, I will be protected from the curse of sin. God has promised me an eternal dwelling place with Him in heaven. He is my shelter and refuge from the world's snares of temporary gratification.

Prayer

Thank You, Father, for the security I have in You. Let me not wander from the protection of Your statutes. Amen.

MARCH 29
DAY 88

I am the true vine, and my Father is the gardener. He cuts off every branch in me that bears no fruit, while every branch that does bear fruit he prunes so that it will even be more fruitful.
JOHN 15:1–2

Pruning a Fallen Tree

Once the tree was on the ground, it was time to cut off all the branches and dead limb stubs from the tree. I cut off everything until I had nothing left but a thirty- to forty-foot log. All I needed to do now, was to cut the log to the lengths I needed for them to become a part of the cabin.

When I first became a Christian, I was like a tree with many dead and useless branches. There were many areas in my life that needed to be cut off. If I walk obediently with God, He promises to cut and prune away the sinful areas of my life so that I will become more like His Son and bear much fruit.

Prayer

Dear Heavenly Father, cut away the areas of my life that are keeping me from producing the spiritual fruit You desire for me to produce. Amen.

MARCH 30
DAY 89

In the same way, on the outside you appear to people as righteous
but on the inside you are full of hypocrisy and wickedness.
MATTHEW 23:28

Good on the Outside, Rotten on the Inside

As I mentioned before, I tried to use all the timber I could that was already on the ground. Some of the trees had fallen over years previously. To my surprise, I was able to get some good logs even though they have been lying for so long. There were times, however, when the log looked good on the outside but was rotten on the inside.

When I first became a Christian, my pastor told me I would meet people who called themselves Christians but whose actions and words did not bear much fruit. I become more aware of people like this the older I get. They go to church and Sunday school but during the other six days of the week they are a rotten testimony for Jesus Christ. The world is watching and if they see no difference, they do not feel the need to receive Jesus.

Prayer

Heavenly Father, reveal any hypocrisy in my life and help me
to change so that I have a strong testimony for You to use in a
lost world. Amen.

MARCH 31
DAY 90

Be completely humble and gentle; be patient, bearing
with one another in love. Make every effort to keep the
unity of the Spirit through the bond of peace.
EPHESIANS 4:2–3

Crossbeams for Roof Support

Just as my first logs resting on mountain stone provide the foundation for the whole cabin, the crossbeams are the main support for the
roof. At this point, it was essential that each crossbeam was level with
one another so that the framing and the pitch of the roof would be
equal on each side. I was particular in picking crossbeams that were
straight and solid because I knew they would play an important role in
the overall strength of the structure.

Jesus is the main foundation, the head or cornerstone of the church.
He is the rock I stand on. I also need support from other believers in
Christ. The family of God needs to be supportive of fellow believers
through the good and bad times.

Prayer

> *Dear Heavenly Father, use me to encourage others in their walk*
> *with You. Thank You for the saints of the past and present who*
> *strengthen my faith in You. Amen.*

APRIL 1

Day 91

Plans fall for lack of counsel, but with many advisers, they succeed.
Proverbs 15:22

Two Heads Are Better Than One

I was sitting on top of the crossbeams when my friend and his son-in-law pulled into the driveway. I was at one of those points in the construction of the cabin where I was not sure what I wanted to do next. The four walls and crossbeams were easy. However, when it came to the roof, I was still undecided on how to frame it and what materials to use. I had all sorts of ideas running through my mind. My friend and his son-in-law both worked in construction. No more than an hour went by before all the details for framing and covering the roof were worked out.

The Bible has many examples of patriarchs, kings, and early Christians receiving wise counsel from one another. Wisdom is more precious than rubies (Prov. 8:11).

Prayer

Dear Heavenly Father, I pray I will never be too proud to seek the wisdom of others and use me to give good counsel when called upon. Amen.

APRIL 2

Day 92

If we have been united with him like this in his death, we will certainly also be united with him in his resurrection.
Romans 6:5

Spring has Sprung

Just as refreshing as that first blast of cool northern air feels after a long hot summer is how the first warm air of spring feels after the short cold days of winter. The snow has melted. The clocks have been turned forward. The fern fiddlers are pushing up through the ground.

The buds on all the trees are getting ready to burst open. God's creation is coming back to life.

Christians celebrate Easter at this time of year. Three days after the crucifixion of Jesus Christ, He rose from the grave just as He had promised. He lives. He gained victory over death. The same victory every believer has in Jesus.

Prayer

Thank you, Heavenly Father, for fulfilling Your promise through the obedience of Your Son Jesus even though it meant His death, and for the life He has given believers through His resurrection. Amen.

⬥

APRIL 3
DAY 93

Every good and perfect gift is from above, coming down from the Father of the heavenly lights, who does not change like shifting shadows.
JAMES 1:17

The Four Seasons

Personally, I feel that northeastern Pennsylvania is one of the best places in the world. I really enjoy the climate and the changing of the four seasons every three months. It seems you no sooner grow weary of one than the transition into the next season is beginning. The long warm days of summer, which lead into the fall spectacle of color, then the short, cold, dormant days of winter, which come back to life with warmer temperatures and sides of mountains blooming with mountain laurel.

I truly do enjoy the changing of the four seasons. However, I am truly grateful that God does not change. He is all-loving, all-knowing, and omnipresent, and His justice cannot be compromised. God is one thing in life I can put all my trust in and never regret doing so.

Prayer

> *Dear Heavenly Father, help me always to trust Your will for me, and let me not put my trust in the temporary fixes the world has to offer. Amen.*

APRIL 4

DAY 94

So, because you are lukewarm—neither hot nor cold—I am about to spit you out of my mouth.
REVELATION 3:16

Cold Spring Water

There is a state park not far from where we live that has a designated swimming area. It could be ninety-five degrees outside but when you jump into that spring-fed swimming hole, the cold takes your breath away. Spring water is always cold. Taking a swim in a spring-fed pool or taking a long deep drink of spring water is a good way to refresh oneself on a hot summer's day.

This is the way God wants my Christian witness to be: either hot or cold. Lukewarm water is susceptible to becoming stagnant and contaminated. If I am a lukewarm Christian, I am susceptible to the woes of the world and the world cannot see the evidence of Jesus in my heart.

Prayer

> *Dear Heavenly Father, help my witness to be refreshing to those who do not know Your Son as their personal Savior. Amen.*

APRIL 5
DAY 95

We live by faith, not by sight.
2 CORINTHIANS 7:13

Spring Scenery

The geese settle on the pond. The bluebirds look for places to build their nests. The plumage of the male yellow finches turns brilliant yellow. All the trees begin to bloom and the grass is turning green. I see more skunks, raccoons, and opossums as they rouse themselves from winter's rest and the male turkeys are strutting for the females. These sure signs of spring can only truly be appreciated with God's gift of sight.

The gift of sight enriches life, but it is not a requirement in my relationship with God. In fact, my sight can be an obstacle for me and lead me to sin. We are to live by faith not by sight. Though the blind man cannot see, he can still experience the redeeming quality of our Lord and Savior Jesus Christ.

Prayer

Dear Heavenly Father, help me to see life through the eyes of Jesus and help me to keep my eyes focused on You. Amen.

APRIL 6
DAY 96

In a flash, in a twinkling of an eye, at the last trumpet. For the trumpet will sound, the dead will be raised imperishable, and we will be changed.
1 CORINTHIANS 15:52

The Sounds of spring

The honking of the geese coming back from their southern habitats announces spring's arrival. Then I begin to notice the different songs of birds at the feeders, such as the robin, the bluebird, and my favorite, the Carolina wren. The one sure sign warmer temperatures are here to stay is the chorus of spring peepers at night, also known as tree frogs or wood frogs. For an animal no bigger than a thumbnail, the noise they make in unison is almost deafening. We actually have to shut the windows some evenings just to have a normal conversation.

God is no stranger to sound. He has often used and will use trumpets to announce His presence. The walls of Jericho fell down at the sound of trumpets and the shouts of His people (Josh. 6:20). We will also hear the sound of trumpets at the second coming of the Lord.

Prayer

Heavenly Father, help me to live each moment of my life as if at any moment I will hear the sounds announcing Your second coming. Amen.

APRIL 7
DAY 97

Her husband has full confidence in her and lacks nothing of value.
PROVERBS 31:11

She speaks with wisdom, and faithful instruction is on her tongue.
PROVERBS 31:26

Seven Crossbeams

I remember the day I put my crossbeams up as if it was yesterday. The first phase of the cabin was complete. The same morning, my wife, Carol, came to see how the cabin was progressing. I showed her the five crossbeams I had ready to be nailed in place. Carol made the suggestion that I should use seven crossbeams for added strength. In my excitement to start framing the roof I took an unwise shortcut. The old adage

"If you are going to do something, do it right or don't do it at all," came to mind. I went with the seven crossbeams and I am glad I did.

Over the years, I have come to learn to listen to Carol when she gives me constructive criticism. The verses from Proverbs 31 perfectly describe her.

Prayer

Thank You, Heavenly Father, for blessing me with my wife, Carol. I am grateful for her wisdom and godliness. Amen.

APRIL 8
DAY 98

And through him to reconcile to himself all things, whether things on earth or things in heaven, by making peace through his blood, shed on the cross.
COLOSSIANS 1:20

Spanning the Gap

The crossbeams added stability to the four standing walls. The beams bridged the gap between the two adjacent walls. They form the foundation for the roof and provide the support needed for the loft. Without the crossbeams, the log cabin could not have been completed.

Without the cross, the plan to restore man to God could not have been completed. The cross bridges the gap between earth and heaven. I like to use this illustration when teaching children during what are called "chalk talks." It is a good visual aide on how God reconnected Himself to mankind.

Prayer

Thank You, Heavenly Father, for fulfilling Your plan and keeping Your promise by providing the cross as a walkway for mankind to come to You. Amen.

APRIL 9
DAY 99

Come to me, all you who are weary and burdened, and I will give you rest. Take my yoke upon you and learn from me, for I am gentle and humble in heart, and you will find rest for your souls. For my yoke is easy and my burden is light.
MATTHEW 11:28–30

Supporting the Weight

Webster's dictionary definition for truss is a structural frame base on the geometric rigidity of the triangle to function as a beam to support a roof. Designing and implementing a truss was the next step in my cabin-building experience. It was the most difficult in design and construction but was the most rewarding when complete. My seven cross beams formed the base of the triangle for the seven trusses I constructed. The trusses needed to be able to support the weight of the corrugated galvanized steel sheets being used for covering the roof.

Sometimes the weight of the world seems like more than I can bear. When I learn to put my trust in Jesus and not in myself, He promises to lighten my burden so that I can withstand the heaviness of my heart.

Prayer

Jesus, I pray that You will always be on the throne of my heart and I will trust You with the burdens of life. Amen.

APRIL 10
DAY 100

When Moses came down from Mount Sinai with the two tablets of the Testimony in his hands, he was not aware that his face was radiant because he had spoken with the Lord.
EXODUS 34:29

Ridgepole

The ridgepole is the backbone of the roof. It runs the length of the cabin and hangs over the edge by a foot in the front. The ridgepole is the highest point on the cabin. It is the peak of the roof. It was not until the ridgepole was in place that I was able to continue the work of framing the roof.

There are times in my Christian life when I have mountain top experiences with God. Moses and Elijah had these types of encounters with God. The mountaintop is a place where I am rejuvenated and my spiritual tank is filled to overflowing. Sometimes it is a weekend conference or a revival meeting or doing a good deed that causes me to feel the overwhelming presence of God. As good as these times with God are, I need to come back down into a lost world.

Prayer

Thank You, Heavenly Father, for those special times with You. Help me to use these experiences to be a better witness to those who do not know You. Amen.

APRIL 11
Day 101

Heaven and earth will pass away, but my words will never pass away.
MATTHEW 24:35

Support Beams

The ridgepole lies on top of seven support beams. I cut each support beam forty-two inches long. I notched out the middle of each crossbeam. Then I stood the support beam in each notch and toenailed it into place. The tricky part was getting everything level. The crossbeams were not perfectly level and the ridgepole was not perfectly straight. Therefore, I had to set the ridgepole on top of the support beams to determine which ones needed to be trimmed. I did this so the ridgepole would set squarely on top of the support beam to obtain maximum support for holding up the roof.

Science, history, and archeology support God's Word. These different areas of academic study prove true to what is written in the Bible. However, even if you took away these supports, God's Word would stand alone from the attacks of those trying to discredit the Bible as God's Word.

Prayer

Heavenly Father, I am grateful that Your Word does not need the proof of man for it to be my manual for daily living. Amen.

APRIL 12
DAY 102

For since the creation of the world God's invisible qualities—his eternal power and divine nature—have been clearly seen, being understood from what has been made, so that men are without excuse.
ROMANS 1:20

Evidence Left Behind

Usually in late March or early April, we have a visitor that passes through some time between when we go to bed and when we wake up. You can usually count on him or her paying a visit the first time temperatures begin to warm up after a long cold winter. If you have not guessed by now, I'll tell you: I am talking about the hungry black bears coming out of hibernation. We do not see or hear them but the knocked-over burn barrel is a sure sign they have passed through. In addition, we usually keep our bird feeders up one day longer than we should and on the morning after we find them strewn across the yard.

I cannot see God but the evidence of His presence is all around me. It is evident in His creation, the testimony of fellow believers, and the Bible. I cannot see the wind but I can feel it and see the effects of its presence. The same is true of God for any person who is genuinely searching to know Him.

Prayer

> *Dear Heavenly Father, help me to have a pure heart so that I can see You clearly (Matt. 5:8). Amen.*

APRIL 13

DAY 103

And the blood of Jesus, his Son, purifies us from all sin…If we confess our sins, he is faithful and just and will forgive us our sins and purify us from all unrighteousness.
1 JOHN 1:7, 9

Hypotenuse

I nailed the roof poles at the end of each crossbeam to the top of the ridgepole. They completed the triangle for the trusses. The crossbeam was the base of the triangle, the support beam for the ridgepole came off the crossbeam at a right angle, and finally the roof pole was the hypotenuse of the right-angled triangle. I do not remember many mathematical formulas but I do remember the formula for calculating the length of the sides of a right-angled triangle: A squared plus B squared equals C squared.

Every person born since the creation of Adam and Eve has a condition that separates them from God. This condition is a sinful nature. God is love and it is not His desire for anyone to be separated from His love, so He has given mankind a formula to restore fellowship with Him by removing the sin. That equation is: repentance and the blood of Jesus equals forgiveness.

Prayer

> *Thank You, Heavenly Father, for the plan of salvation. Thank You for providing humanity a way to have personal fellowship with You. Amen.*

APRIL 14
Day 104

*And pray in the Spirit on all occasions with all kinds
of prayers and requests. With this in mind, be alert
and always keep on praying for all the saints.*
Ephesians 6:18

Roof Pole Braces

After all the roof poles were up, I had fourteen right-angled triangles
forming the trusses for my roof. For added support, I braced up the roof
poles. I came in two feet from the end of each crossbeam and nailed in
an eighteen-inch brace. I now felt comfortable that the roof poles had
the extra support they needed. They also provided me with a place to
nail the sideboards for my loft.

As missionaries leave their home churches to fulfill the Great
Commission (Matt. 28:16-20) Jesus has given them, they need our
support in a variety of ways. Sending money, prayers, and Christian
materials and writing letters are just some of the means by which we
can be a blessing to those reaching others for Christ.

Prayer

> *Heavenly Father, as I leave the doors of my church help me
> to be a missionary wherever I go and convict me to support
> missionaries in their work for You. Amen.*

APRIL 15

DAY 105

This is the meaning of the parable: The seed is the word of God. Those along the path are the ones who hear, and then the devil comes and takes away the word from their hearts, so that they may not believe and be saved…But the seed on good soil stands for those with a noble and good heart, who hear the word, retain it, and by persevering produce a crop.
LUKE 8:11–12, 15

Boards on Top of Roof Poles

I only had one more thing to do to the roof frame before I could cover it with the three-foot by eight-foot sheets of corrugated galvanized steel. I nailed one-inch by ten-inch by twelve-foot hemlock boards on top of the roof poles. Starting at the top and working my way down, I nailed boards across lengthways at two-foot intervals. After this job was done, I now had a place for the roofing nails to grab hold.

As a Christian I need to try my best to be sensitive to the opportunities God gives me to share His love with those around me. It is essential for me to sow seeds of God's love every chance I get. It is not for me to worry whether the seeds will fall on fertile soil and grab hold; all I can do is pray that some of the seeds will embrace the Word of God, and in turn produce fruit.

Prayer

Thank You, Heavenly Father, for the prayers and words of those who lead me to the Lord. I pray that those who do not know You will take hold of the cross I carry for You each day (Luke 9:23) so they may know you personally. Amen.

APRIL 16
DAY 106

*But store up for yourselves treasures in heaven, where moth and
rust do not destroy, and where thieves do not break in and steal.
For where your treasure is, there your heart will be also.*
MATTHEW 6:20–21

Galvanized Steel

I was not sure what material I wanted to use for roofing. I was
thinking about tying down a plastic or canvas tarp. After thinking about
it for several weeks and listening to the advice of others, I finally made
a decision. My cabin's roof would be covered with three-by-eight foot
sheets of corrugated galvanized steel. Durability and resistance to rust
were two of the major attributes that attracted me to this material.

Anything man-made is eventually subject to corrosion. So many of
the things I pursue are only temporary pleasures. That is why Jesus tells
me to store up my treasures in heaven where moths and rust cannot
destroy them.

Prayer

*Dear Heavenly Father, I pray that my endeavors on earth will
be worthy of heavenly storage, protected from the curse of decay
on the world. Amen.*

APRIL 17
DAY 107

*In addition to all this, take up the shield of faith, with which
you can extinguish all the flaming arrows of the evil one.*
EPHESIANS 6:16

Shielded from Rain

When I first started construction, I honestly did not know whether I was going to build a cabin or a pavilion. I knew only that I wanted to build something to replace the twelve-by-twelve screened-in tent that had been destroyed by the weight of the snow. I wanted to build a structure with a roof large enough to protect everyone from sudden summer showers.

Satan is relentless in trying to make me doubt my faith. He wants me to compromise my beliefs with the other beliefs of the world. He knows the power I have through God, so he is constantly trying to diminish my effectiveness. God has given me the shield of faith. If I use this part of God's armor effectively, it will protect me from the devil's downpour of temptations.

Prayer

> *Dear Heavenly Father, I pray that my shield of faith will protect me from Satan's fiery darts. Help me to stand firm in my faith (1 Cor. 15:58). Amen.*

APRIL 18
DAY 108

Then Jesus said to his disciples, "If anyone would come after me, he must deny himself and take up his cross and follow me. For whoever wants to save his life will lose it, but whoever loses his life for me will find it."
MATTHEW 16:24-25

Cost of the Roof

Up to this point, the cost of the cabin was minimal. The only cost so far had been for nails, and that was less than twenty dollars. I did not want to cut any corners on the roof, so I did not make price an issue when I bought the materials I needed. I purchased twelve sheets of galvanized corrugated steel, galvanized roofing nails with rubber washers, and the roof cap. It cost me eighty dollars to get the cabin under a roof.

God paid the price for my sins through the death of His Son Jesus Christ. When I accepted Jesus as my Savior, I did not realize what it would cost me. I had to die to self in order to grow more Christlike. I would be hated by the world, which meant alienation from past so-called friendships and ridicule from members of my family. I need to bear my cross daily to be a true follower of Jesus (Luke 9:23).

Prayer

Dear Heavenly Father, I pray that I will make the daily payments necessary to walk closer with You. Amen.

APRIL 19
DAY 109

What shall we say, then? Shall we go on sinning so that grace may increase? By no means! We died to sin; how can we live in it any longer?
ROMANS 6:1–2

The Roof Slope

My friend and his son-in-law helped me to determine what the slope should be on the roof. Their one idea was that if the slope was steep enough I would have enough headroom to put in a loft where two people could sleep. I had never considered this option but now I added it to my mental blueprint. They also said the slope should be steep enough that the snow would slide off when the metal roof heated up in the winter sun.

I know there are different thoughts on this belief but I believe you cannot lose your salvation if you are truly saved. I do sin and it is my prayer that the Holy Spirit will convict me of my sin so I will repent. The word "backslide" cannot be found in the New Testament. However, there are times when I take a step backwards in my faith. I cannot allow a sin to become a habit in my life. Sin prevents me from having the fellowship God desires to have with me.

Prayer

I pray that I would not backslide in my faith and that I will be able to help a brother or sister who has made some bad decisions. Amen.

APRIL 20
DAY 110

*Two are better than one, because they have
a good return for their work.*
ECCLESIASTES 4:9

A Helpful Hand

The cabin I was building was a personal project. It was something I wanted to do on my own. However, when it came to putting on the roof I was very glad for the day my friend came to give me a hand. With his experience in construction, he helped me square up the first sheet on each side. Then we snapped a line for a starting mark for the rest of the sheets. He held the bottom of the sheet while I lined up the top to the snapped line and drove home the roofing nails. I am positive the roof would not have turned out as well if my friend had not been there to guide me.

The Bible tells us that two are better than one. As much as I like my time alone, it is good to fellowship with others. We need other believers to be uplifted and to share our spiritual gifts with one another.

Prayer

Thank You, Heavenly Father, for the friends You have given me. Help me be a blessing to others in their time of need. Amen.

APRIL 21

DAY 111

For to me, to live is Christ and to die is gain.
PHILIPPIANS 1:21

Holes in the Roof

It seems to me there should be another technique for putting on a roof other than putting holes in it with nails. The last thing I wanted was for the roof to leak. After I had the sheets of steel in place, it was difficult for me to pound a hole in them with a nail. However, I used the correct nails with rubber washers and nailed them in the correct locations. I am happy to report that to this date I have had no leaks in the roof.

The Bible tells me that I need to die to live (2 Tim. 2:11). When I first read these words, I did not understand them correctly and it did not sound like something I wanted to do. Kind of like putting holes in the roof with nails. However, after the Holy Spirit revealed to me that I needed to die to self and let Jesus live and have control of my life, it made perfect sense.

Prayer

Dear Heavenly Father, help me to keep self off the throne of my heart and let Jesus be in complete control of everything I do, say, and think. Amen.

APRIL 22

DAY 112

*In fact, everyone who wants to live a godly life
in Christ Jesus will be persecuted.*
2 TIMOTHY 3:12

The Correct Spot

The first piece of corrugated steel was in place and ready to be nailed down. If you do not know what corrugated means, just imagine what a three-by-eight-foot ruffled potato chip would look like. I was ready to nail in the low spot when my friend said, "Don't nail there; you want to nail it down on the high side." When it rains the water runs down the low ripples of the steel, so if there are no nails there it will be less likely to leak. The only problem, it was more difficult to nail down the sheet of steel. Nailing on the high side you had to hit the nail several times before it pierced the steel.

Doing the right thing is not always easy. This was especially true for me during my adolescence and young adult years when the need to fit in and be part of a group seemed so important. There will be many times as a Christian when the things I say and do will go against people.

Prayer

> *Heavenly Father, help me to stand firm on my Christian convictions and when my faith is questioned by the world, even though it may be more difficult, let me use these opportunities to be a witness for You. Amen.*

APRIL 23
DAY 113

He then began to teach them that the Son of Man must suffer many things and be rejected by the elders, chief priests and teachers of the law, and that he must be killed and after three days rise again.
MARK 8:31

Pounding Nails through Steel

I had a pouch full of roofing nails and my hammer in hand. I was ready to start securing the steel sheets to the roofs nailing boards. By the end of the day, the roof was complete. I felt very gratified to have the roof done but I also felt the sharp pain in my thumb and index finger from holding the nails in place while trying to pound them through steel.

Pain is part of being human. From headaches to muscle aches we all experience different degrees of pain throughout life. In Mel Gibson's movie *The Passion of the Christ,* he depicts the suffering of Christ during His scourging and crucifixion very graphically. I can only imagine the suffering Christ endured on my behalf.

Prayer

Dear Heavenly Father, help me to detest sin with the same passion as You do even to the point of allowing Your Son to suffer at the hands of man. Amen.

APRIL 24
DAY 114

Everyone who competes in the games goes into strict training. They do it to get a crown that will not last; but we do it to get a crown that will last forever.
1 CORINTHIANS 9:25

Roof Cap

We finished the roof in a day. All eight sheets of steel were secured to the nailer boards. Where the two sheets met at the peak of the roof there was a fourteen-foot long gap that needed to be covered. They make a roof cap that covers this seam in the roof. I purchased a ten-foot section and fabricated the remaining four feet I needed to cut down on the cost. The roof cap is the crown on top of the roof. It was the final addition that waterproofed the inside of the cabin.

God's Word refers to crowns that Christians will receive in heaven. The only jewelry I wear is my wedding ring and I cannot see myself wearing a crown. It is my hope, however, to complete the plan God has for me, making me worthy of receiving the crown of life (Rev. 2:10).

Prayer

Heavenly Father, I can only imagine the glory You have in store for me in my heavenly home. Let me live my life on earth in a way to be worthy of all Your heavenly blessings. Amen.

APRIL 25

DAY 115

Blessed are they whose transgressions are forgiven, whose sins are covered.
ROMANS 4:7

Covered by the Roof

It was a beautiful sunny day when the roof went on. This was the only part of building the cabin with which I needed help. My friend who has experience in construction came over and helped me. I am very glad he was there. He not only helped me handle the awkward three-by-eight-foot sheets of corrugated steel but he kept me from making a mistake in squaring up the roof. At the end of the day, the roof was up. Now I could even work on the weekends it rained. I could work inside and be protected by the covering of the roof.

The blood of Jesus has covered the transgressions of my heart. The blood of Jesus protects me from the punishment of sin. My Heavenly Father sees me through the blood of His Son Jesus and I am justified in His eyes.

Prayer

Heavenly Father, I will be forever grateful for the power of the precious blood of Jesus that covers all of my iniquities. Amen.

APRIL 26

DAY 116

But the LORD said to Samuel, "Do not consider his appearance or height, for I have rejected him. The LORD does not look at the things man looks at. Man looks at the outward appearance, but the LORD looks at the heart."

1 SAMUEL 16:7

Cabin Frame

With the sheets of galvanized steel in place and the gable ends soon to be covered with one-by-twelve-inch planks of hemlock, the framework for the cabin trusses would no longer be visible. The appearance of the cabin improved greatly once the framework was no longer visible. However, if the trusses were poorly built and not up to the task of supporting the outer covering, the improved appearance would be short-lived.

One of my favorite verses in the Bible is 1 Samuel 16:7, when God tells Samuel the prophet who is choosing Israel's second king that the heart of a person is more important than their outside appearance. It is sad but true from the world's perspective, people with good looks get better jobs and receive more attention.

Prayer

Heavenly Father, keep me from judging a book by its cover. Help me to see the inner beauty of a person's heart. Amen.

APRIL 27
DAY 117

*Therefore, if anyone is in Christ, he is a new
creation; the old has gone, the new has come!*
2 CORINTHIANS 5:17

From Logs to Boards

It was time to cover the gable ends. I went to the sawmill and purchased one inch by twelve inch by twelve-foot planks of rough-cut hemlock. I got the boards with some splits in them to cut cost. The lumber for the gable ends and the loft was my second biggest expense. The bill was sixty-five dollars including the nails. Sawmills are one of the few places to find work in Sullivan County. The sawmills transform any type or size of log into lumber which then can be used for a variety of purposes.

It is God's desire to transform mankind so that we can be used for His glory (Rom. 12:2). There is no sin too great that the blood of Jesus Christ cannot cut through it. When I accepted Jesus as my personal Savior, I became a new creation. I was reconciled to my Heavenly Father and became a vessel He will use for the plan He has for me.

Prayer

Dear Heavenly Father, help me to keep my new vessel clean of sin so I can be used by You to share the love of Your Son, my Lord and Savior Jesus Christ, with those I encounter each day. Amen.

APRIL 28
DAY 118

I have hidden your word in my heart that I might not sin against you.
PSALM 119:11

Closing in the Gable Ends

The four walls were up and the roof was on. The only other major construction left was to close in the gable ends. I was able to accomplish this task in one day. I started with the bottom board and worked my way up to the peak. With each board I put into place, I overlapped the previous board by an inch. Therefore, when all the boards were in place not only did it look great but it was also an effective barrier against wind and rain.

I must never forget I am in a spiritual battle against Satan and his demons. They are tireless in their efforts to render me ineffective for God's purposes. The Son of God knew this and when Satan tempted Him, He used His Father's Word to defeat those attacks (Matt. 4:1–11). When I memorize God's Word it remains in my heart and when needed is an effective barrier against the spiritual temptations of Satan.

Prayer

Heavenly Father, I pray that You would give me a discerning heart so I will be aware of the subtle attacks of Satan, and can defend myself with Your Word hidden in the recesses of my heart. Amen.

APRIL 29

DAY 119

Blessed are the pure in heart, for they will see God.
MATTHEW 5:8

Measure Twice

I used my carpenters' ruler to figure the angle I needed to cut my hemlock planks to fit the slope of the roof. I unfolded five sections of the ruler. I held three of the sections on the bottom straight edge with the other two unfolded to match the angle of the roof. I held the ruler securely so not to lose my angle as I transferred it onto my one inch by twelve inch plank. I am sure everyone who has done a little carpentry work has heard the old adage "measure twice, cut once."

There are times in my Christian life when I ask myself if what I am doing is pleasing to God. Unlike the carpenters' saying, if I have to think twice to know if something is pleasing to God, chances are the activity is probably compromising my Christian walk.

Prayer

Dear Lord, I pray that each breath I take will be a blessing to you so with a pure heart I will clearly see my Heavenly Father. Amen.

APRIL 30
DAY 120

I will bless them and the places surrounding my hill. I will send down showers in season; there will be showers of blessing.
EZEKIEL 36:20

Rain on a Tin Roof

Now that I had the roof on and the gable ends closed in, I was looking forward to a rainy day. I enjoy the sound of raindrops splashing on a tin roof. It is one of those noises that make you want to sit a little closer to the woodstove with a good book. This is just one of the countless blessings I was looking forward to enjoying while spending time out at the cabin.

God truly does shower us with His blessings. If I have trouble falling asleep, I start counting my blessings from the breath I take to the stars in the sky. I always fall asleep before I run out of blessings.

Prayer

Dear Heavenly Father, thank You for Your goodness and help me to be grateful and content with Your blessings in my life. Amen.

MAY 1
DAY 121

*The rain and the snow come down from heaven, and do not return
to it without watering the earth and making it bud and flourish,
so that it yields seed for the sower and bread for the eater.*
ISAIAH 55:10

Spring Splendor

Spring is a beautiful time of year. Where I live it usually takes until
the second or third week in May until all the plants are in full bloom.
The azaleas, wild cherry trees, and apple trees are the first to blossom.
Then you know it will not be long before the rest of the plants around
the house and the wild flowers in the woods and field show their
splendor (Matt. 6:28-29).

It was a wise person who coined the phrase "Take time to smell
the roses." Everyone should take the time to fill his or her senses with
the beauty of God's creation. It is amazing to me the colors and the
blending of colors, which make up the different patterns in flowers. God
truly reveals Himself through His creation. I am glad I have reached a
place in my life where I appreciate His handiwork.

Prayer

*Thank You, Heavenly Father, for the daily reminder of Your
presence through the beauty of Your creations. Amen.*

MAY 2
DAY 122

*In the same way, let your light shine before men, that they
may see your good deeds and praise your Father in heaven.*
MATTHEW 5:16

Taking Notice

The further along I got on my cabin, the more people started to
notice the progress I was making. My wife, who knows my carpentry
skills, was a little skeptical at first, but after she saw the frame of the

roof completed, she became a believer. Our friends also watched the progress of each week's work on the cabin. Even my neighbor stopped by the day I was nailing on the metal roof. His words were, "I had to come over and see what all the racket was about."

I am very aware of the world watching my Christian walk. They will be the first to let me know when I stumble. Their comment will be, "I thought you were a Christian, Christians shouldn't do that." It is amazing how non-Christians take notice of what a Christian should or should not do.

Prayer

Heavenly Father, I pray that my Christian walk would be a reflection of Jesus, so that I may have an opportunity to witness to observers how You saved me from my sins. Amen.

MAY 3
Day 123

For everything in the world—the cravings of sinful man, the lust of his eyes and the boasting of what he has and does—comes not from the Father but from the world. The world and its desires pass away, but the man who does the will of God lives forever.
1 John 2:16–17

Warm Weather Activities

With the arrival of spring comes an increase in outdoor activities. Grass is cut weekly, weeds are pulled and sprayed, and the wood supply for next year's winter is cut. With the warmer weather, I can wash our vehicles at home instead of going to the car wash, and homeowner maintenance such as caulking, painting, and cleaning the siding of the house can be done. Let us not forget the sneaking in of a little turkey hunting and trout fishing. Along with all these other activities, I still kept my schedule for building the cabin.

As I get older, the activities of life seem endless. Family, job, volunteer work, marriage, and hobbies all have their places in my daily life.

There are days I needed to tell myself the busyness of life could not take away from my daily devotional time I need to have with God.

Prayer

> *Heavenly Father, no matter how hectic life becomes remind me always to put You first and everything else will fall into place. Amen.*

MAY 4
DAY 124

At that time if anyone says to you, "Look, here is the Christ!" or, "There he is!" do not believe it. For false Christs and false prophets will appear and perform great signs and miracles to deceive even the elect—if that were possible.
MATTHEW 24:23–24

Turkey Hunting and Trout Fishing

Springtime is the perfect time of year for those people who enjoy hunting and fishing. In Pennsylvania, spring turkey season is underway. You can hunt from one half hour before sunrise until noon. That lets all afternoon and evening for the individuals who enjoy fishing for trout. I use a fly rod in trying to catch trout. I cast out an imitation of an insect hoping to trick a hungry trout into believing it is the real thing. Earlier in the day while spring gobbler hunting, I tried to imitate the call of a hen to draw the attention of a lovesick tom.

The Bible warns us of false prophets. There are people who are wolves in sheep's clothing (Matt. 7:15). Unfortunately, many people are led astray and will perish eternally because of the false messages they are hearing. The best way I can defend myself from false teachers is to know God's Word.

Prayer

> *Dear Lord, give me a discerning heart so that I will know a false prophet when I encounter one. Amen.*

MAY 5
DAY 125

"Isn't this the carpenter? Isn't this Mary's son and the brother of James, Joseph, Judas and Simon? Aren't his sisters here with us?" And they took offense at him.
MARK 6:3

Working with Wood

When I have the time I do enjoy being creative. I like working with wood as a medium. My Dad is very artistic and shared his talents with me when I was a young boy. Whether it was pencil drawing or building a dog box, I was often by my father's side watching and learning. Today I enjoy whittling animal figures out of pieces of basswood or carving designs on walking sticks. I would definitely not consider myself a master craftsman. In the world of construction, I would be more apt to doing the rough lumbering rather than the finishing work.

I do not think of it often since it is not spoken of much in the Bible, but our Lord and Savior was a carpenter by trade. I am sure Joseph taught him well and Jesus listened to his instructions intently. I am grateful for Jesus' example of being obedient to His parents (Luke 2-51).

Prayer

Thank You, Heavenly Father, for allowing me to be raised by loving parents who took the time to share their talents with their son. Amen.

MAY 6
DAY 126

*Here I am! I stand at the door and knock. If anyone hears my voice
and opens the door, I will come in and eat with him, and he with me.*
REVELATION 3:20

Door Handle

I had the handle I was going to use for the cabin door early on in
the construction of the cabin. I found a piece of driftwood, bent in
the shape to make a perfect handle. I laid the piece of wood on my
workbench where it remained for months. Then finally, the time came
when I was able to make a reality of what I was only imagining months
before. I cut my handle close to the angle it needed to be; I then took
it to work and sanded both ends until they were equal. I put the handle
on with wood screws and wood glue. I now have a rustic handle for
opening the door of the cabin.

My spiritual heart also has a door that needed to be opened. When
I was twenty-five years old, I finally heard Jesus knocking and knew I
needed to let Him in. I finally realized the need to be free from sin and
have Jesus in control of my life.

Prayer

*Dear Lord, I am forever grateful that You continued to knock
at the door of my heart until I let You in. Thank You for all
You did and are doing in my life. Amen.*

MAY 7
DAY 127

*I am the gate; whoever enters through me will be saved.
He will come in and go out, and find pasture.*
JOHN 10:9

Doorway

I could have left the entrance to the cabin open. It still would have served its purpose as a pavilion and protection if we had to get out of the rain while picnicking. The only problem was every other creature of the forest could take up residence, especially during the winter months when not being used. I decided to put on a door to keep out all animals bigger than a mouse while providing an entrance for those allowed in.

God cannot have sin in heaven. Since everyone is born with sin, God needed to provide a way for man to have his sin washed away. He did this through the crucifixion of His Son Jesus Christ. Jesus is the door I must go through in order to enter into the sinless place called Heaven.

Prayer

Thank You, Heavenly Father, for providing a doorway for mankind to enter into fellowship with You. Amen.

MAY 8
DAY 128

The animals going in were male and female of every living thing, as God had commanded Noah. Then the LORD shut him in.
GENESIS 7:16

Latches on the Door

I have two latches on the cabin door, one for the outside and one for the inside. The latches keep the cabin door shut. When I leave the cabin, I latch the door on the outside and when I turn in for the night, I latch the door on the inside. This prevents the wind or unwanted four-legged visitors from opening the cabin door. It is up to the person leaving the cabin or the last one to bed to latch the door.

There is going to come a day when the doorway to heaven will be shut (Matt. 25:10–11). God shut the door to Noah's ark and only saved the people within. God's grace will not always be available. Today is the day to go through the door God has provided through His Son Jesus Christ. Do not wait until tomorrow because the door may be shut.

Prayer

Dear Heavenly Father, I pray for those who have not yet gone through the doorway of heaven before their opportunity is closed. Amen.

MAY 9
DAY 129

But the Counselor, the Holy Spirit, whom the Father will send in my name, will teach you all things and will remind you of everything I have said to you.
JOHN 14:26

Door Jam

The width of the door was one inch. I framed out the opening for the door with the two-by-fours inset one inch so when the door was closed it would be flush with the outside of the cabin wall. The door jam serves two functions. One, it prevents the door from swinging into the cabin; and second, it stops the wind from coming straight through the sides of the door.

Jesus did not leave me defenseless during my pilgrimage on earth. He sent the Holy Spirit to help me along the way. The Holy Spirit has several functions: He is my comforter and counselor, He helps me understand God's Word, and He intercedes with the Heavenly Father when I do not have the words to express my needs.

Prayer

Thank You, Jesus, for sending me the Holy Spirit. I pray that I will be sensitive to the Holy Spirit's activity in my life. Amen.

MAY 10
DAY 130

For prophecy never had its origin in the will of man, but men
spoke from God as they were carried along by the Holy Spirit.
2 PETER 1:21

Inspiration for the Door Design

It took me a while to decide on what design to use for my door. One design I considered seriously was to have the door hinged at the top. When you pushed or pulled the door open it would remain open by the support of two six-foot poles hinged at the bottom, and it would act as a canopy. I decided against this design because of the issue of weight and only people strong enough could open the door. The door I finally built was inspired by one I saw on a cabin in a movie.

Every word in the Bible is inspired by God. Man's hands may have written it, copied it, and translated it into different languages but the true author is the Holy Spirit. God's words are flawless (Prov. 30:5). I can depend on God's word to guide me through the decisions of life.

Prayer

I am grateful for the Word of God. I am thankful that I have a book that documents the love my Heavenly Father has for me. Help me to share Your Word in such a way that other people will come to know You personally. Amen.

MAY 11
DAY 131

Let us draw near to God with a sincere heart in full assurance
of faith, having our hearts sprinkled to cleanse us from a guilty
conscience and having our bodies washed with pure water.
HEBREWS 10:22

Fitting the Door into the Door Jam

Making the door jamb and building the door were easy projects. The hard part would be hanging the door so it would close correctly onto the door jamb. You could not have any tight spots or the door would not close and I did not want any gaps to let in mice or the cold winter air. My door jamb was one and a half inches thick so the door had to fit within a half inch for a nice fit. As I cut the door to size, I tried my best to get as close as possible to the measurements I needed.

God wants me to try my best to be obedient to His statues. The closer I walk with God the more intimate my relationship with Him will be. I need to fit God into everything I do.

Prayer

Heavenly Father, no matter how routine my life sometimes seems to be, let me do everything in such a way that my walk will be nearer to You. Amen.

***

MAY 12

DAY 132

"Do not be afraid of those who kill the body but cannot kill the soul. Rather, be afraid of the One who can destroy both soul and body in hell."
MATTHEW 10:28

Killing Frost

The propane heaters still kick on this time of year. Back in 1977, this area received several inches of snow. My nephew and I were camping this time of year in 2006 when one morning it got down to thirty-two degrees. It seems every year in May we get several weeks of warm weather which brings out the apple and azalea blossoms in full display, and then suddenly we get a killing frost. The frost kills the blooms but the tree or shrub will continue to grow.

The Bible warns me that I do not have to fear those who can kill my body but not my soul. However, I do need to be afraid of our adversary

Satan who can kill both my body and my soul. It is Satan's desire for me to spend eternity with him in hell.

Prayer

> *Dear Heavenly Father, give me the conviction I need to understand the severity of Satan's deception so that I will have the compassion to witness to those who are lost. Amen.*

MAY 13
DAY 133

For God so loved the world that he gave his one and only Son, that whoever believes in him shall not perish but have eternal life.
JOHN 3:16

Door Hinge

The cabin door was extremely heavy. I contemplated for several months on how I was going to hang the door. I visited the local hardware store and looked at their biggest hinges. They were a little pricey, and I was not even sure if they would sustain the weight of the door. I was explaining my dilemma to some of the guys at the machine shop and they suggested I make my own hinges. I stayed late one Friday and proceeded to cut, drill, and weld until I had four extraordinarily heavy-duty hinges, which I was confident would hold the weight of the door.

I can always be confident that God's love for me will never fail. He loved me first (1 John 4:19). He loved me so much that He sent His only Son to die on the cross for my sins. His love is extraordinary and is sometimes hard for me to fully understand.

Prayer

> *Thank You, Heavenly Father, for the love You have for me. I pray that I will be able to share that same love with each person that crosses my path. Amen.*

MAY 14

DAY 134

*But grow in the grace and knowledge of our Lord and Savior
Jesus Christ. To him be glory both now and forever! Amen.*
2 PETER 3:18

Mountains Turning Green

I was coming home from work when I looked at the mountains, and it was as if overnight they had turned green with their new foliage. While out turkey hunting the third Saturday of the season, I also noticed how green the forest was getting. Every shade of green you can imagine is on display this time of year. From the ferns on the ground to the tops of the trees and everywhere in between was green.

When I taught for Childhood Evangelism Fellowship, I used a wordless book to help reach children for Jesus. Instead of words on the pages, the five pages of the book were a different color. Gold for God, black for sin, red for the blood of Jesus, white for our sins being washed away, and green for the need to grow in our faith. So even today, when I see plants and trees turning green in the spring, it reminds me of the need for me to grow in my relationship with Christ.

Prayer

*Heavenly Father, allow me to have the desire to become more
Christlike. Your work is never finished in me. Help me not to
interfere with the growing process. Amen.*

MAY 15

DAY 135

*Let us rejoice and be glad and give him glory! For the wedding
of the Lamb has come, and his bride has made herself ready.*
REVELATION 19:7

The Doors Threshold

The definition for threshold is the sill of the doorway, or the entrance to a house or building. I made my cabin's threshold out of a four-foot log. I then took my chainsaw and cut lengthways three inches down from the top and bottom giving me a flat surface on both sides. I was very careful not to cut the length too short. I wanted a snug fit against the bottom logs of the cabin. As it turned out I had to use my sledgehammer to get my threshold in place, then I toe nailed it in to keep it there.

Whenever I hear the word threshold, I always think of the groom carrying his bride over the threshold. It also reminds me the church is the bride of Jesus. Some day I will gather for a wedding feast in heaven with the Lamb of God. Just as the groom carrying his bride over the threshold symbolizes a new life together as one, the church and all its members are one with Jesus.

Prayer

> Dear Heavenly Father, help me to love my wife as Jesus loves the church (Eph. 5:25) and the church to remain faithful to Jesus. Amen.

MAY 16
DAY 136

In the same way, let your light shine before men, that they may see your good deeds and praise your Father in heaven.
MATTHEW 5:16

Sunlight through the Windows

The walls were up, the roof was on, and the door was hung. The cabin was beginning to look just like I imagined from the outside. On the inside, however, when the door was closed, it was dark even on the brightest of days. The interior of the cabin needed illumination. On both sides of the cabin I installed windows. This allowed the sun to brighten the inside.

The Son of God brought light into a dark world (John 8:12). I need to let my light shine in a dark world. Where there is darkness, people cannot see the truth. Allow me to share the light of life to those living in darkness so they too can see the truth and change from within.

Prayer

Dear Heavenly Father, I pray my spiritual fire will burn brightly, so I will be effective in penetrating the darkness of the world, and bring others into the light. Amen.

MAY 17
DAY 137

"The LORD has kept the promise he made: I have succeeded David my father and now I sit on the throne of Israel, just as the LORD promised, and I have built the temple for the Name of the LORD, the God of Israel."
1 KINGS 8:20

Windows Can Break

Boys breaking a window some time during their childhood is a common occurrence. I can remember two that I broke. The most infamous was the windshield of a just washed and waxed car the day of my sister's wedding.

In the pines where my cabin is built there are dead limbs that fall to the ground on windy days. I am concerned that some day one of these airborne limbs will break one of the windows in the cabin. To date I am happy to report that no windows have been broken.

I am even happier when I recall that God has never broken a promise. Parents, friends, relatives, and acquaintances sometimes have to go back on promises they have made. With God I can rest assured that any promise He has made will come to pass (Heb. 10:23), including the return of His Son Jesus Christ.

Prayer

Thank You, Heavenly Father, for never breaking a promise You have made. It gives me great hope in the promises yet to be fulfilled. I pray that I will be careful not to make promises I can't keep. Amen.

MAY 18
DAY 138

On this day atonement will be made for you, to cleanse you. Then, before the LORD, you will be clean from all your sins.
LEVITICUS 16:30

Clean Windows

My wife and I have a general rule when it comes to chores. She does inside and I do the outside work. One of my outside responsibilities includes cleaning the windows. I do this three to four times a year.

On my way to work, I drive along side the Loyalsock creek. Certain times of year I drive through insect hatches that leave my windshield in dire need of being cleaned. Either the reason for a window is to see through or let light in, which means, they need to be kept clean.

My heart needs to be kept clean so I can see God (Matt. 5:8). When my heart is blackened with sin, I need to clean it by asking for forgiveness. The more holy my life, the closer my fellowship with God will be.

Prayer

Heavenly Father, it is my desire to have a pure heart to see You more clearly. Please convict me of any sin in my life so I can ask for forgiveness and have it washed away. Amen.

MAY 19
DAY 139

"For I was hungry and you gave me something to eat,
I was thirsty and you gave me something to drink,
I was a stranger and you invited me in."
MATTHEW 25:35

The Glow From Within the Cabin

One of my favorite Christmas cards is that of a snow-covered cabin with a wreath on the front door, smoke coming out of the chimney and a yellow glow coming through the windows. There is something very inviting with that scene. It makes you curious to know what is going on inside the cabin. I want to go inside and be part of the activities, especially the holiday meal I imagine is being prepared. The thought of duplicating this picture was just another reason for me to stay on my cabin-building schedule.

This is how my Christian witness should be to those in the world. I want people to look at me and say to themselves, I want to know what is going on inside of that person. I want to know what makes that person so content, patient, and joyful.

Prayer

Heavenly Father I pray that the glow of Your unconditional love will be evident in my life in a way to attract those who don't know You, giving me the opportunity to share Your Good News with them. Amen.

MAY 20
DAY 140

Choose my instruction instead of silver, knowledge rather than choice gold.
PROVERBS 8:10

Deciding What Chimney to Build

Decisions, decisions, decisions; deciding what style chimney to build was as challenging as deciding the design for the whole cabin. My first thought was to build a fireplace and chimney with mountain stone. The further I studied the details of doing this the more I realized my time constraints and my masonry prowess would not allow me to build a stone fireplace. Then when my one friend offered to donate a wood-burning stove with glass windows in the doors and another friend offered triple-lined stovepipe, my decision was made for me.

God wants me to make wise decisions. When Moses had to make a tough decision, he prayed. I often think of Moses as an example when I need to decide what to do. When making a decision the first thing I do is go to God for guidance and direction. I do not want to make a decision in pursuit of greed and I need to be content with what I have and use what God have given me for His glory.

Prayer

Dear Heavenly Father, I pray that both the conscious and unconscious decisions I make each day would be according to Your will for my life. Amen.

MAY 21
DAY 141

*There let us stop passing judgment on one another.
Instead, make up your mind not to put any stum-
bling block or obstacle in your brother's way.*
ROMANS 14:13

Free From Obstructions

In choosing the site for my cabin, I took several things into consideration. Where I was going to put the chimney was one of them. Would
the chimney be made of stone or stovepipe? Even before I laid the first
log, I knew I had to take into consideration the space and clearance
the chimney needed. I certainly did not want my chimney running up
against the trunk of a tree or having it run up through a bunch of tree
branches. I wanted to stay clear of any obstacles.

As I walk in my daily Christian life, I need to stay clear of situations
that may cause me to sin. I have to avoid obstacles in my life that cause
me to stumble. Likewise I don't want to obstruct my fellow Christian's
path to God with temptations in those areas of there life where I know
they are weak.

Prayer

*Heavenly Father, Satan knows where I am weakest, and his
desire is to cause me to stumble in my walk with You. Help
me to walk around his obstacle course and straight into Your
arms. Amen.*

MAY 22
DAY 142

"He cuts off every branch in me that bears no fruit, while every branch that does bear fruit he prunes so that it will be even more fruitful."
JOHN 15:2

Cutting the Hole for the Wood Stove

The roof is complete, the door is hung, and the windows are in. The next project on my list is the installation of the wood stove. This would be my last alteration to the cabin walls. I had to cut a four-by-five-foot hole in the bottom center of the back wall. I am always tentative when it comes to starting up the chainsaw and cutting a hole in a perfectly good wall. It was, of course, something that had to be done to complete the project.

Sometimes I feel uncertain when God asks me to step out of my comfort zone. I do not want to change or get out of my routine, but God knows what is best for me so I can become more like His Son. I have to be willing to let God reshape me into the person He desires to carry out the plan He has for me.

Prayer

Dear Heavenly Father, help me to be submissive when You have to cut unwanted traits out of my life so I can become the person You desire me to be. Amen.

MAY 23
DAY 143

Instead, be filled with the Spirit. Speak to one another with psalms, hymns and spiritual songs. Sing and make music in your heart to the Lord.
EPHESIANS 5:18–19

Filling the Hole with Mountain Stone

I really like the look of mountain stone when used for building walls, fireplaces, and chimneys. Since time and expertise did not allow me to build a stone fireplace and chimney, I had to compromise with my original idea. This is the reason I made the hole as big as I did just for a stovepipe to go through. I wanted to fill the four-by-five-foot hole with mountain stone. This gave me the desired look I was picturing in my mind.

When I became a Christian, I become a new creation in Christ (2 Cor. 5–17). The time used for old sinful habits needed to be replaced. God's Word tells me I need to be filled with the Holy Spirit. The Holy Spirit will help me to attain the desired characteristics God is looking for.

Prayer

Heavenly Father, help me to fill every void in my life with an activity pleasing to You. Amen.

MAY 24
DAY 144

*The blessing if you obey the commands of the LORD your God
that I am giving you today; the curse if you disobey the commands
of the LORD your God and turn from the way that I command
you today by following other God's, which you have not known.*
DEUTERONOMY 11:27–28

Mountain Stone (a Farmer's Curse, a Mason's Blessing)

There many things Sullivan County does not have in abundance. Mountain stone would not be included on this list. When my wife asks me to plant something outside, I cringe because I know I will need a digging iron to remove the mountain stone that lies six inches under my covering of grass. There are fence rows of mountain stone from farmers clearing their fields. If you are a mason and enjoy making rock walls and stone chimneys, Sullivan County would be paradise.

When Adam and Eve disobeyed God, they brought the curse of sin into the world. Death entered the world and they needed to work for their sustenance, which still affects us today. However, I can still receive God's blessing. By receiving Jesus as my personal Savior, I can have victory over the bondage of sin.

Prayer

*I am grateful, Heavenly Father, that You took a fallen sinner
and through the cleansing power of Jesus Christ's shed blood,
made what was once unworthy useful for Your glory. Amen.*

MAY 25
DAY 145

Man's anger does not bring about the righteous life that God desires.
JAMES 1:20

Separating Logs from a Hot Stove Pipe

I could have bought a stovepipe insulator to run my stovepipe through the log wall just as I have for my wood-burning stove on the porch. I would have only had to cut one log to install it. Two things kept me from going this route. One, the cost of the insulator; and second, I like the look of mountain stone. The mountain stone was plentiful, free, and it works great in separating the logs from the hot stovepipe.

It is very rare when man's anger is an act of righteous indignation. My anger should never be out of control and never displayed in a way that would adversely affect my witness to the world. The Bible warns me to separate myself from hot-tempered individuals (Prov. 22:24) and admonishes the Christian to be slow to anger and quick to listen (James 1:19).

Prayer

Dear Heavenly Father, help me to stop when I see red so I am able to keep my emotions in control so You can be in control. Amen.

MAY 26
DAY 146

Because of the increase of wickedness, the love of most will grow cold, but he who stands firm to the end will be saved.
MATTHEW 24:12-13

Hot Mountain Stone

I associate the words *damp* and *cold* with castles and stone basements with dirt floors. In most circumstances when you find mountain stone, it is cool to the touch. However, if it is close to a source of heat such as a wood-burning stove it will absorb the heat like a sponge. It takes a while for the stones to warm up, but once heated up they keep the cabin warm even after the fire has gone down.

As a Christian, I have to be very careful not to let the godlessness of the world cause my heart to grow cold. I need to stay close to the source of love to maintain the desire to share the gospel with all nations. Even when I am not having a mountaintop experience, my heart will still radiate the love of God to those around me.

Prayer

Heavenly Father, help me not to become discouraged by the world's coolness towards You. Rather, let my witness help lost hearts warm up to Your goodness. Amen.

MAY 27
DAY 147

For the law appoints as high priests men who are weak but the oath, which came after the law, appointed the Son, who has been made perfect forever.
HEBREWS 7:28

The Sun (God's Perfect Source of Heat and Light for Man)

God in His infinite wisdom gave us the sun to warm our days and give us light to see. I am at that age where I need to use reading glasses to help me to see. But it amazes me that even on a cloudy day when I need to read something without my glasses, I can see well if I use the light of the sun by a window rather than the artificial light of a lamp. The light of the sun is perfect. It has the full spectrum of rays within it.

I am glad that the Son of God is perfect. He became man and lived a sinless life. Through His example, I can have victory over the temptations I face each day. Jesus was without defect, which enabled Him to be worthy of sacrificing Himself for our sins (1 Pet. 1:19).

Prayer

Thank You, Heavenly Father, for Jesus Your perfect Son. Through Him, I have eternal life. Help me to see You clearer through the eyes of Your Son Jesus. Amen.

MAY 28
DAY 148

The LORD detests the sacrifice of the wicked, but the prayer of the upright pleases him.
PROVERBS 15:8

Smoke Rising Up to Heaven

I could not wait to see smoke coming out of the chimney. No sooner did I have the chimney cap secured than I tested to make sure I had a good draft up the chimney. I crumpled up a piece of newspaper, lit it and ran outside to see the result. No sooner did I step outside than there it was—the picture I had in my mind was now a reality. The smoke from my cabin chimney was curling heavenward.

God has the same desire for the members of His family to send up prayers to heaven. I should be praying continually (1 Thess. 5:17). God wants to be in the forefront of all my thoughts, words, and actions.

Prayer

Dear Heavenly Father, I pray that my daily walk with You would be a living prayer that rises before Your heavenly throne and is pleasing in Your sight. Amen.

MAY 29
DAY 149

To them God has chosen to make known among
the Gentiles the glorious riches of this mystery,
which is Christ in you, the hope of glory.
COLOSSIANS 1:27

A Sign of Hope

Smoke rising from a chimney has had a comforting affect on many an observer, especially if the smoke is rising straight up to the sky. This is a sign of good weather to come. When inclement weather is on the way, and the wind starts blowing, the smoke rolls out and goes to the side. I can imagine, though, that no matter which direction the smoke was heading out of the chimney, it brought instant hope to many a weary traveler. Smoke from a chimney would mean somebody was probably home, it would be warm inside, and possibly a hot meal was prepared.

I am so glad for the hope I have in Christ. I cannot imagine living life without Christ and with the hopelessness the world has to offer. With Christ, each day brings expectation just knowing God is in control of the plan He has for my life. Even if that day takes me through the doorway of death, I am promised eternal life.

Prayer

Thank You, Heavenly Father, for the hope You bring to me
each day. Help me to bring that same hope to those I encounter
who are living each day pursuing temporary desires. Amen.

MAY 30
DAY 150

"Be strong and very courageous. Be careful to obey all the law my servant Moses gave you; do not turn from it to the right or to the left, that you may be successful wherever you go."
JOSHUA 1:7

The Chimney Ladder

The wood-burning stove in the cabin is only used when temperatures force us inside; otherwise, we sit around the fire outside. To prevent birds, squirrels, and other critters from building nests in the chimney when the wood-burning stove is not in use, I plugged the top with a clay flowerpot. It fits the hole just right, leaving me enough exposed on top to easily remove. I had to build a chimney ladder so I could climb up to put in or take out the flowerpot when needed.

Ladders always remind me of the world's idea of success. "Climbing the ladder of success" is a cliché often used to describe someone who is aspiring to reach the top of his or her profession. Some people will do whatever it takes to reach the top rung of that proverbial ladder. God wants me to succeed but more importantly He wants me to obey Him in all that I do while I am getting there.

Prayer

Dear Heavenly Father, let me see success through Your eyes. Help me to be content with all Your blessings, and as I climb upward let me become more Christlike along the way. Amen.

MAY 31
DAY 151

You are my lamp, O LORD; the LORD turns my darkness into light.
2 SAMUEL 22:29

Darkness into Light

I will never forget the first time I lit the kerosene lanterns inside the cabin. My friend and I were sitting around the campfire outside of the cabin. I had the cabin door open so we could look in. It was a satisfying moment to see the inside of the cabin illuminated. The actual sight was far better that what I imagined. It was dusk and grew darker as we sat around the fire. The neat thing was, the darker it got outside the brighter and better it looked inside the cabin.

Most activities that are displeasing to God are done under the cover of darkness or where they cannot be seen by others. Light exposes what activity is taking place in the dark. There are even sunshine laws for elected officials to abide by so they do not make decisions and leave the public in the dark. I need to be the light in a dark world so others might see their errors, come to Jesus, and ask for forgiveness.

Prayer

Heavenly Father, I pray that Your Son will shine brightly in my life so I can see clearly the obstacles of sin in a dark world. Amen.

JUNE 1
Day 152

And she gave birth to her firstborn, a son. She wrapped
him in cloths and placed him in a manger, because
there was no room for them in the inn.
Luke 2:7

Room to Rest

I have to thank my friend for the idea to build a loft. With his experience in construction, it was his suggestion to make the peak of the roof high enough to have room for a loft. Before his suggestion, I was going to have the slope of the roof just great enough for rainwater to run off. Now not only would rainwater run off but also snow would slide off when the tin roof heated up, and I would have room to sleep without taking up the limited space I had available.

Jesus left His glorified home to be born in a manager because there was no room for Mary and Joseph at the inn. I need to make room for Jesus in my heart. I need to let Him in so He can have complete control of my life.

Prayer

Dear Heavenly Father, I pray that my witness to others would help them to realize the importance of making room for Jesus in their lives. Amen.

JUNE 2
Day 153

"The Son of Man did not come to be served, but to
serve, and to give his life as a ransom for many."
Matthew 20:28

Making Added Space

Before I built the loft, I was limited to the floor space I had in the lower level. To make the loft I used the one-by-twelve-inch rough-cut hemlock leftover from building the gable ends. The planks were laid on top and nailed down to five of the seven crossbeams. This allowed a person who was six feet tall or less plenty of room to stretch out. The two exposed crossbeams were directly above the wood-burning stove. This allows the heat to rise unimpeded on cold winter nights so all slumbering guests are kept warm. I nailed planks to the side and front to keep restless sleepers in place. When completed the loft gave me an added sixty square feet of floor space.

God wants me to make room in my life not only for Jesus but also for people I encounter each day. I desire to have a servant's heart. Through an encouraging word or deed, I want to try my best to meet the needs of others.

Prayer

> *Heavenly Father, give me the ability to see the needs of those around me. Then, help me make room in my life to meet those needs. Amen.*

JUNE 3
Day 154

I have hidden your word in my heart that I might not sin against you.
Psalm 119:11

Storage Space

The floor space in the cabin not including the loft is approximately one hundred square feet. In that space, there is a stove, table, shelves, benches, rocking chair, wood and wood stove utensils. This leaves me enough room to move about while doing cabin chores. It would have been a little cramped if it were not for the loft. The extra sixty square feet in the loft gave me not only room to sleep but also the room I needed to store clothes and gear while using the cabin to hunt.

God not only wants me to make room for Jesus and others in my heart, He wants me to store His Word in my heart. God knows that His Word is my greatest defense against my enemy Satan. After all, what better example do I need than when Jesus resisted Satan's temptation while fasting in the desert by using His Father's Word (Matt. 4:1–11). Satan is a defeated foe and cannot stand up against the truth of God's Word.

Prayer

Heavenly Father, I pray that I will make a lifelong commitment to storing Your Word in my heart, so I can recall those words of truth when I need to fight off temptation or make decisions. Amen.

JUNE 4
DAY 155

He who dwells in the shelter of the Most High
will rest in the shadow of the Almighty.
PSALM 91:1

Sleeping on a Soft Pad

My wife would be the first to tell you that I can sleep anytime, anywhere. All I need is a fifteen-minute power nap to be re-energized. Now the idea of sleeping a full night in a sleeping bag on top of rough-cut hemlock boards is a different story. I purchased two foam pads to lie on to improve the comfort of my sleeping area. Along with my pillow, I manage to get a full night's sleep and wake up refreshed.

If I let the business of worldly pursuits encompass my life, it does not take long for anxiety levels to rise up and fatigue to set in. It is imperative for me to have a daily quiet time with God. I pray continually throughout the day for His guidance, and I make time for fellowship with other believers once a week. If I do these things and obey God's commandments, I am comforted knowing I am in fellowship with my Heavenly Father.

Prayer

> *Dear Heavenly Father, thank You for providing me with a place where I can come to find rest from the business of daily routines. Amen.*

JUNE 5
DAY 156

In the same way, on the outside you appear to people as righteous but on the inside you are full of hypocrisy and wickedness.
MATTHEW 23:28

Fly Fishing/Fly Fisherman

Changing the oil in my car does not make me an auto mechanic any more than putting a band-aid on a cut makes me a doctor. I believe the same is true for fly-fishing. Fly-fishing is one of the few activities I pursued while working on the cabin. In my opinion, just because you are fishing with a fly rod does not make you a fly fisherman. I fished with a fly rod for thirty-three years, but it was not until I spent a ten-hour day on Penn's Creek that I became a fly fisherman. What I learned that day and the passion I felt forever changed my perspective towards fly-fishing.

Just because I go to church every Sunday does not make me a Christian. Every Sunday churches are full of people who just go through the motions. On the outside, they might look like a Christian but on the inside, their hearts have never been changed. They need to have that special day when they truly believe and become a new creation in Christ Jesus.

Prayer

> *Heavenly Father, I pray for all those individuals who are masquerading as Christians. I pray for a day when they will truly be spiritually born again. Amen.*

JUNE 6
DAY 157

"And besides all this, between us and you a great chasm has been fixed, so that those who want to go from here to you cannot, nor can anyone cross over from there to us."
LUKE 16:26

Filling in the Gap

At this point of construction my cabin would be good for getting out of the rain, however it would not keep you warm in cold weather, even with wood burning in the stove. The reason for this was that I had not yet chinked the cabin. With my logs not being of equal diameter and having to notch each log differently to keep the walls level from side to side, I had anywhere from zero to five-inch gaps between the logs. Filling in the gap between each log with a chosen material is called chinking.

There is also a great divide between God and man caused by sin. God used His son Jesus to reconcile man and God (2 Cor. 5:18). For Christians that void has been filled through the cleansing blood of Jesus. God's desire for me is to testify to the world of His love to mankind through Jesus so the gap between God and man will be nonexistent.

Prayer

Help me, Lord, to love the world. Help me to fill the void in people's hearts with the knowledge of Your saving grace. Amen.

JUNE 7
DAY 158

Therefore, my dear brothers, stand firm. Let nothing move you. Always give yourself fully to the work of the Lord, because you know that your labor in the Lord is not in vain.
1 CORINTHIANS 15:58

Tedious Work

The time came to choose the material I would use to chink. Several options came to mind, one being the traditional use of chicken wire and mortar, or nailing planks on the inside to cover the gaps between the logs. I decided against both of these ideas due to the cost. I finally decided to use various sizes of mountain stone pointed with mortar to fill in the gap. I knew the job ahead was going to be very tedious but the finished appearance would be well worth the effort.

My life is filled with the daily routines. As a Christian though, I can look at each day with expectancy. Every phone call and every chore I do is an opportunity to glorify God. I cannot let the tedious details of life make me feel ineffective for God's work. I can strive to grow more Christlike each day with God in control of my life.

Prayer

Dear Heavenly Father, every breath I take has a reason in Your eyes. Let me use the daily routine of life to be a faithful servant used by You. Amen.

JUNE 8
DAY 159

When Moses' hands grow tired, they took a stone and put it under him and he sat on it. Aaron and Hur held his hands up—one on one side, one on the other—so that his hands remained steady till sunset.
EXODUS 17:12

Rocks Supporting Rocks

It took approximately fifty to sixty rocks to fill in one gap between each log, with each rock being as important as the next. I usually started the process by picking one stone that would fill the gap tightly. I would then begin the process of wedging various sized rocks against one another to fill the entire gap between the two logs. Each rock or pieces of rock were needed to support the rock beside, above or below it.

I need the support of others in my pursuit to live a victorious Christian life. Just as Moses needed the help from Aaron and Hur to gain victory over the Amalekites by holding his arms up, I need prayer support and accountability partners to help me gain victory over areas of weaknesses in my life.

Prayer

Heavenly Father, I pray that I will surround myself with fellow Christians who will hold me tight to my convictions of living a pure and holy life. Amen.

JUNE 9
DAY 160

All your words are true; all your righteous laws are eternal.
PSALM 119:160

No Loose Stones

When it came time to secure the loose rocks in place, I used my hammer to wedge rock against log or rock against rock. I had to hit each rock hard enough to wedge it in place but not so hard as to loosen the rock previously in place. Each rock had to be secure. I could not tolerate any loose stones. Each rock had to be firmly in place so when I pointed with mortar it would remain in its place.

I hear the word *tolerant* being used a lot today. The world tries to make me feel guilty by saying that if I truly love someone I will accept him or her as they are, and I need to accept alternative life styles chosen by individuals. If I do not I am labeled judgmental and uncompassionate. What is right for me does not necessarily mean it is right for someone else. The world believes in moral relativism where the Christian believes in absolute moral truth. God cannot tolerate sin.

Prayer

> *Dear Heavenly Father, help me not to compromise Your standards with the world's. Give me the compassion to love those living loose moral lives. Amen.*

JUNE 10
DAY 161

A fool spurns his father's discipline, but whoever heeds correction shows prudence.
PROVERBS 15:5

Warning Signal of the Mosquito

Where I live, we are not overwhelmed with mosquitoes or black flies. With a little bit of insect repellant you can usually ward off any insect bites. The swarms of black flies and mosquitoes are one thing that would keep me from moving to Alaska and some of the other northern woods. I can remember backpacking in Glacier National State Park in Montana with friends, and at night we were confined to our tents because of the mosquitoes. There is nothing more annoying to me than the buzzing of a mosquito at your ear. At least they give you a warning signal before trying to eliminate them.

All through life there are warning signals. Do not touch, stay off, no trespassing, slippery when wet, to name just a few. The wise man heeds the warning signals he encounters each day. I also need to listen to the warning signals of the Holy Spirit when He is trying to keep me from sinning.

Prayer

> *Heavenly Father, help me to hear the voice of the Holy Spirit
> so that I can eliminate sin from my life. Amen.*

JUNE 11
DAY 162

*I know your deeds, your love and faith, your service and persever-
ance, and that you are now doing more than you did at first.*
REVELATION 2:19

A Good Draft is Essential

One of the main reasons I did not build a stone fireplace was the design of the flue. Building a fireplace with a chimney was a lot more complex than I thought. It is not simply a stone box with a smokestack on top. From the books that I read, the length, width, and height of the firebox had to be in proportion to the hole of the chimney and the back of the flue needed to be angled. Unless everything was just right, I would have a poor draft, which meant a smoky cabin instead of the smoke going up and out of the chimney.

Just as a good draft is essential for a smoke-free room, there are qualities that are essential for a healthy church. There is no church or denomination in the Christian faith that is perfect. How many times have you heard someone say, I do not go to church because it is full of hypocrites? Jesus is the only one who claimed to be perfect. The rest of us are works in progress, but if we abide by the qualities described in our reading today, we will come out of church and be an effective witness to the world.

Prayer

> *Heavenly Father, I pray that Your church will continue to be a blessing to those in need physically, mentally, and spiritually throughout the world. Amen.*

JUNE 12
DAY 163

After this I heard what sounded like the roar of a great multitude in heaven shouting: "Hallelujah! Salvation and glory and power belong to our God."
REVELATION 19:1

Thunderstorms

In the latter part of spring, weather conditions are often favorable for producing thunderstorms. With the hot humid air rising and colliding with an oncoming cold front, it is a recipe for some dynamic weather conditions. As the thunderheads form, you can hear the rumbling in the distance and the lighting flash across the sky. Living in the mountains the sound of the thunder is accentuated as it echoes off the sides of the hills and rolls through the valleys. At times, it will clap so loud it will actually rattle the windows of the house.

As a child, I remember my parents' explanation for the sound of thunder. For every explanation I received the one thing that always remained true is God being included. Thunderstorms always remind me of God's awesome power. With the wind blowing, the thunder clapping, and the lightning flashing, I cannot help but look up and think of God.

Prayer

> *Dear Heavenly Father, I pray that as thunderstorms come and go, even the unsaved would think of You, which would begin*

the process of repentance and a personal relationship with You. Amen.

JUNE 13
DAY 164

My guilt has overwhelmed me like a burden too heavy to bear.
PSALM 38:4

Humidity

My wife and I would have made good Eskimos. If you gave us our choice of either winter or summer, we would both pick winter. We do not like the heat and humidity of summer. When conditions are like that, chances are we will be inside enjoying the air-conditioning. Fortunately, where we live we will only get one or two weeks of ninety degrees with high humidity. The word *close* is a word we use in the area to describe the feeling of oppression one gets during days of high humidity.

The feelings of guilt I get from sin can also lead to oppression. It may not be guilt but troubles I face in my life that make me feel closed in or backed into a corner. Whenever I start feeling like this, I need to find refuge in the Lord.

Prayer

Heavenly Father, help me to be quick to repent of sin and let me turn to You when situations begin to heat up to a boiling point. Amen.

JUNE 14
DAY 165

When we were overwhelmed by sins, you forgave our transgressions.
PSALM 65:3

Do Not Look at the Whole Job

I was not sure I chose the wisest method for chinking the cabin. When I looked at the whole cabin and all the chinking that needed to be done, I felt overwhelmed. There were twenty-eight ten foot long gaps that needed to be filled. My first concern was finding enough stone the right size to fill each gap and secondly lodging each stone in place. If I only concentrated on one gap at a time, the job did not seem unattainable.

As a Christian living in the world, there are also times when I feel overwhelmed trying to live a holy life. Satan does his best to convince my flesh of what I need to live a fulfilled life. I have to remind myself that the things of this world cannot replace the joy by being obedient to Jesus. When I do stumble and sin, I must quickly ask for forgiveness from a God who is quick to forgive and forget my transgressions.

Prayer

Help me, Heavenly Father, to be content with Your daily blessings, and not to be anxious or inundated with what the entire world has to offer. Amen.

JUNE 15
DAY 166

He called his twelve disciples to him and gave them authority to drive out evil spirits and to heal every disease and sickness.
MATTHEW 10:1

Choosing the Right Stones

With my pile of stones beside me, I started to fill in the gaps between the logs. It was like putting a jigsaw puzzle together. I had to pick through the pieces and look for the right shape. There was nothing special about any one stone but each stone was equally as important as the one it supported. I did not go to a stone quarry to buy special stone. I used the mountain stone I found on our property.

Jesus did not go to the school for training Pharisees to pick the brightest students to be His twelve apostles. As He traveled through Galilee and the surrounding area, He chose ordinary men to be the ones to advance His heavenly kingdom. The same is true today. I do not need a special degree to be part of the family of God. God wants me to use the talents I have to spread the good news.

Prayer

Thank You, Heavenly Father, for loving each one of us just as we are. Help me to see others through Your eyes and love them as You love me. Amen.

JUNE 16
DAY 167

I praise you because I am fearfully and wonderfully made; your works are wonderful, I know that full well.
PSALM 139:14

Original Idea for Chinking

I depended on books and advice from others to help me with the construction of the log cabin. However, when it came time for chinking, I went with my own idea. Trying to build the cabin with as little monetary input as possible is what truly inspired the idea of using mountain stone and pointing with mortar to fill the gaps in between the logs. I have never seen a log cabin chinked in this fashion. It truly is unique and pleasing to the eye.

The Bible tells me that God wonderfully created me in the hidden place of my mother's womb. Every person is unique. God has a special plan only I can fulfill if I am obedient to God. God made me with talents and gifts that He wants me to use to reach others for the Kingdom of God.

Prayer

Thank You, Heavenly Father, for the diversity in each believer. Help me to use my uniqueness to meet the needs of my brothers

*and sisters in Christ and to reach out to those in rebellion
towards You. Amen.*

JUNE 17
DAY 168

*However, I consider my life worth nothing to me, if only I may
finish the race and complete the task the Lord Jesus has given
me—the task of testifying to the gospel of God's grace.*
ACTS 20:24

Keeping on Schedule

When I chose mountain stone and pointing with mortar for chinking
the cabin, I was a little concerned with staying on schedule. I had a
month to get the mountain stone in place and then a month to point
the stone with mortar. When I have big tasks to accomplish, I break
them down into little bite-size portions. I was able to fill a gap in an
hour. With twenty-eight gaps to fill, I knew I needed twenty hours to
accomplish the task. The longer days of summer helped me to complete
this feat easier than I expected.

By staying the course, I was able to finish what I started. God wants
me to stay the course as I live out my Christian life. He wants me to
finish the work started the day I received Jesus as our personal Savior.

Prayer

*Dear Heavenly Father, I know there will be days when I
feel spiritually depleted. Help me to stay the course so I will
complete the work You have for me. Amen.*

JUNE 18
DAY 169

*Finally, brothers, we instructed you how to live in order to
please God, as in fact you are living. Now we ask you and
urge you in the Lord Jesus to do this more and more.*
1 THESSALONIANS 4:1

Practice Makes Perfect

It was a Saturday when I started chinking. I was second-guessing my
chosen method for chinking after the first row took over an hour and
a half to do. However, like anything, the longer you do something the
better you get at it. As the day wore on, I established a technique for
choosing the correct stone and tapping it into place. By the end of the
day, I had one whole side of the cabin completed. As I stood back to
evaluate my day's work, I really liked what I saw.

The longer I walk with Jesus as my personal Savior, the more Christlike I become. It is easier for me to avoid temptations and be obedient
to God, and I have a keener awareness of others' needs. At the end of
each day, I hope my Heavenly Father will also be pleased with what He
sees in my spiritual growth.

Prayer

*Heavenly Father, help me to build up the body of Christ as
I grow in faith and knowledge of Your Son. Let it always be
my desire to live my life in a way that will be pleasing to You.
Amen.*

JUNE 19
DAY 170

For me to live is Christ and to die is gain.
PHILIPPIANS 1:21

Dying With Your Boots On

One evening we were invited along with another couple over to our neighbors' house for supper and games. During our conversation at dinner, the husband of the other couple, who is retired, asked our host, who is in his early seventies, when he was going to retire. I will never forget his reply: "I would rather die with my work boots on than die in a nursing home." It meant a lot to me because I was only forty-nine years old at the time and did not see retirement as part of my plans.

Whether I retire from my trade or place of employment, in my latter years of life God never expects me never to retire from being a Christian. If anything, when and if I retire I will have more time to fine-tune my spiritual tools to be used for God's glory.

Prayer

Dear Heavenly Father, I pray I will learn from the wisdom and testimony of those who have gone before me and You would use the elderly in our church and the time they have to be a blessing to others. Amen.

JUNE 20
DAY 171

O God, you are my God, earnestly I seek you; my soul thirsts for you, my body longs for you, in a dry and weary land where there is no water.
PSALM 63:1

Drink Plenty of Water

I played organized football from third grade up to my graduation from high school. I played back when coaches thought needing a drink of water was a sign of weakness. Now, thanks to a better understanding of our physical needs while doing strenuous activities in the heat, most everyone understands the need for our bodies to be replenished from their loss of fluids. During the summer when I am outside working on the cabin, cutting grass, or getting firewood, I usually have a bottle of water with me.

As a created being in the image of God, my soul has a desire to know God. Like many people, I tried to fill that yearning with activities the world has to offer. However, like many sport drinks that do not quench your thirst like pure cold water, the world will never be able to fill my spiritual void for God. My soul is thirsty for God, and can only be quenched when I take time to fellowship with Him.

Prayer

Dear Heavenly Father, I pray that my heart will constantly yearn for Your fellowship and that I take the time each day to meet with You to restore my spiritual needs. Amen.

JUNE 21
DAY 172

"Have you not put a hedge around him and his household and everything he has? You have blessed the work of his hands, so that his flocks and herds are spread throughout the land."
JOB 1:10

A Barrier from the Cool Damp Ground

The cabin floor was still covered in wood chips and pine needles on top of protruding mountain stones. It was time to decide what type of flooring to put in. I needed something to separate campers' sock-covered feet from the damp forest floor. I thought of using wood but to get the floor level I would lose limited ceiling height. So once again, I used the material at hand, mountain stone.

In our scripture today, Satan implies God had a protective barrier around Job. Early in my Christian walk I heard the expression, "hedge of thorns" used in prayer when praying for an individual. Meaning, God would place a protective barrier between those in our prayers and Satan's deceptions.

Prayer

> *Dear Heavenly Father, I pray for Your protection in the areas of my life where Christian growth is needed and I am vulnerable to Satan's attacks. Amen.*

JUNE 22
DAY 173

He stilled the storm to a whisper; the waves of the sea were hushed.
PSALM 107:29

Smooth Stone for the Floor

I raked the cabin floor clear of all pine needles and wood chips. After this, I removed the mountain stone sticking out of the ground. After clearing the floor I began my search for the biggest and flattest mountain stone I could find that was no more than two inches thick. Sometimes I would find one large rock that was layered. With my mallet and stone chisel, I was able to split the layers and get two to three smooth-surfaced stones.

I tried to make the floor as level as possible, but it was unrealistic to expect perfection when using uneven rocks. It is also unrealistic for me to think everything in my life is going to go smoothly after receiving Jesus as my personal Savior. Living in an imperfect world and being imperfect myself, I know mistakes will be made. Everything will not always go as I expect. However, if I put my trust in Jesus, He can calm the storms in my life. Knowing He is in control gets me through my most difficult trials.

Prayer

> *Thank You, Heavenly Father, for smoothing out my life even when everything around me is in chaos. Amen.*

JUNE 23

DAY 174

Filled with the fruit of righteousness that comes through Jesus Christ—to the glory and praise of God.
PHILIPPIANS 1:11

Filling in the Cracks

After several days of searching, I finally accumulated enough mountain stone to complete the floor. I started laying the stone in the back corner of the cabin. I determined the highest spot on the floor and chose my rocks accordingly. In the low spots I would choose thicker stones and possibly add a little fill while in the high spots I would choose the thinner stones and scrap some dirt away. As I laid each stone, I tried my best to make them level with one another and filled in underneath so the stones would not wobble. Finally, when the floor was complete I swept crushed stone in the cracks followed by sand.

It does not take long for all the little concerns I have in my daily routine to fill up my day. I have to be careful not to allow the little things to fill my time leaving me no time for God. Like putting the crushed stone in before the sand, I need to put God first, and everything else will still fit into my schedule.

Prayer

> *Heavenly Father, no matter how important or time-consuming my responsibilities are for any given day, let me not use them as an excuse not to spend time with You. Amen.*

JUNE 24

DAY 175

*The law was added so that the trespass might increase. But
where sin increased, grace increased all the more.*
ROMANS 5:20

Weeds in the Driveway

Each summer, one chore I know that will be waiting for me is the
task of pulling weeds from the driveway. We have a dirt driveway,
which inevitably has weeds growing in it. Every time I take the dogs for
a walk, I will take the time to pull out some crab grass. This helps but
it usually takes several applications of weed killer to keep the driveway
weed free. If weeds are not dealt with in a timely manner, they will take
hold and completely cover the length of the driveway

When I sin against God, it also needs to be dealt with in a timely
manner. I need to ask for God's forgiveness immediately. Then I need to
take the steps necessary to keep me from sinning in that area of my life
again. Sin like weeds has a way of multiplying. If thoughts are not dealt
with, they can lead to sin (James 1:14–15). If I let the roots of temptation take hold, they will lead me to rebel against God.

Prayer

> *Heavenly Father, the mind is the soil where sin takes hold.
> When tempted, let me turn to You for strength, and when I
> do sin, I pray I will ask forgiveness to keep me sin-free in Your
> eyes through Jesus. Amen.*

JUNE 25

DAY 176

"My command is this: Love each other as I have loved you."
JOHN 15:12

Breaking Stones to Fit in Place

I was not particular when I picked up mountain stone for chinking. As long as it was not too big, I knew it would fit somewhere in the gap. I looked like I was a member of a chain gang with my pile of rocks and hammer in hand. I used my mallet to break up some of the rocks to give me a wide variety of shapes and sizes. Some of these pieces had sharp edges, making them useful in wedging rocks tightly together.

There are times when I need to remind myself of my true calling in life. God wants me to love others with a servant's heart. Even though large chunks of my time are dedicated to work, school, family, and sleep, I need to take the little pieces of time that God gives me to be a blessing to others. A kind word or a loving smile can change someone's outlook for an entire day.

Prayer

Heavenly Father, help me to be keenly aware of the needs of others. Give me the wisdom to fulfill those needs with the unconditional love of Jesus. Amen.

JUNE 26

DAY 177

"Here is a boy with five small barley loaves and two small fish, but how far will they go among so many?"
JOHN 6:9

Small Rocks Are Important

It took all sizes of stone to fill the gaps in between the gaps of the logs. The larger mountain stones filled in the greatest percentage of area between the logs. However, even though the smaller pieces of rock did not fill much space, the role they served was equally important.

All members of God's family are important. God can use a little to accomplish much. Just look at the miracle of the feeding of five thousand. I am sure the small boy that packed five loaves and two fish for lunch did not feel very significant in the large crowd. However, Jesus used the small boy and the little he had to feed the entire crowd. Likewise, He can also use what little I have to offer.

Prayer

> Dear Heavenly Father, help me never to feel insignificant in Your eyes. Let me use whatever it may be to be a blessing to my brothers and sisters in Christ and to those in the world. Amen.

JUNE 27
DAY 178

And the God of all grace, who called you to his eternal glory in Christ, after you have suffered a little while, will himself restore you and make you strong, firm and steadfast.
1 PETER 5:10

Support Cables for the Chimney

From the ninety-degree elbow at the bottom of the chimney to the top of the chimney cap is ten feet. The stovepipe is a foot away from the cabin logs. The air between the stovepipe and the logs is an effective insulator from the heat of the stovepipe burning the logs. I used mountain stone to support the pipe coming from the stove to the outside of the cabin, so it could hold the weight of the ten-foot section of chimney. To keep the chimney from moving side to side I used support cables.

Every day is a new opportunity for me to walk closer with God, which is the last thing my adversary wishes for me to do. I need to remain steadfast in my daily obedience to God. I need the support of Christians through their fellowship and prayers, and quiet time in reading God's Word to keep me from swaying back and forth between worldly philosophies and desires.

Prayer

Heavenly Father, I pray that I will live each day for Your glory. Help me to remain steadfast in my walk with You. Let me not waver under the weight of the world's temptations. Amen.

JUNE 28
DAY 179

Finally, brothers, whatever is true, whatever is noble, whatever is right, whatever is pure, whatever is lovely, whatever is admirable—if anything is excellent or praiseworthy—think about such things.
PHILIPPIANS 4:8

Chimney Cap

I have two chimney caps. The purpose of both is to keep the chimney free from unwanted debris. One cap came with the chimney. It covers the top of the chimney but there is still a ten-inch space between cap and chimney to allow the smoke to draw out. This cap keeps rain, snow, leaves, and twigs from getting into the chimney. My bigger concern was the possibility of having animals building a nest inside the chimney. I had a clay flowerpot that fit the opening of the chimney perfectly. This left me feeling confident the chimney would remain clutter free.

My mind is the battleground for living Godly lives. Temptation starts in the mind. There is a children's song that has the lyrics "Input, output, what goes in is what comes out." I need always to try to keep my mind clean of the clutter and trash of the world. If I fill my mind with worldly images, my mind will burn with worldly desires. I need to fill my mind with thoughts that keep Satan from building strongholds that will render me spiritually ineffective.

Prayer

> *Dear Heavenly Father, help me to keep my mind clear from the world's rubbish. Let me be quick to rebuke Satan when the seeds of temptation enter my thoughts. Amen.*

JUNE 29
DAY 180

Pay attention and listen to the sayings of the wise; apply your heart to what I teach.
PROVERBS 22:17

Allergic Reactions

When I lived in Lancaster, Pennsylvania, I had hay fever. I was pleasantly surprised the first spring after moving to Shunk that my allergies did not flare up. However, this past summer I had two allergic reactions that quickly caught my attention: once when I was stung by a white-faced wasp while mowing the grass. My neck and sides started to itch. Fifteen minutes later, I could no longer withstand the itchy feeling I was experiencing. I ran into the garage, stripped down, and saw I was covered in hives. Fortunately, a cool bath, Benadryl, and air conditioning relieved my condition and the hives left as quick as they came. Secondly, I was enjoying a steak and lobster dinner at our neighbor's house when shortly thereafter, my eyes started to water and my nose was running like a faucet. Now I pay particular close attention to stinging insects and shellfish on the menu.

God has a way of getting my attention and He will not hesitate to rebuke me when I disobey (Rev. 3:19). He does this so that I will be quick to repent of my sin. He also wants me to pay attention to the wisdom of those who have gone before me, so I do not make the same mistakes in my life.

Prayer

> *Thank You, Heavenly Father, for loving me so much that You will rebuke me when I go astray. Give me the wisdom to learn from others so I can avoid the many pitfalls of this world. Amen.*

JUNE 30
DAY 181

The day of the Lord is near for all nations. As you have done, it will be done to you; your deeds will return upon your own head.
OBADIAH 1:15

Days Getting Shorter

My Dad is in his eighties and says his favorite day of the year is the first day of winter. The reason being is that each day after winter the days get longer. Then in three short months, we turn the clocks forward to give us longer and warmer days that help loosen up his stiff muscles.

Well the opposite is true for my wife and me. Our favorite day is the first day of summer, which after each day starts getting a little shorter. We enjoy the cooler temperatures and longer evenings of standard time.

No matter whether you like daylight savings time or standard time, the simple fact remains that there are only twenty-four hours in each day. The older I get the faster days turn into weeks and weeks into years. I've heard it said, "No matter what you did yesterday you traded it for one day of the rest of your life." There is also the saying, "This is the first day of the rest of your life." One fact is certain: After each day I am one day closer to my physical death or the second coming of Christ, and keeping this in mind I need to glorify God with each breath I take, for I don't know when it will be my last.

Prayer

> *Heavenly Father, enable me to utilize the precious gift of the time You have given me, and to use it for Your glory. Amen.*

JULY 1
DAY 182

For everything in the world—the cravings of sinful man,
the lust of the eyes and the boasting of what he has and
does—comes not from the Father but from the world.
1 JOHN 2:16

Filling in the Voids

Now that the chinking with mountain stone was complete, the cabin took on a completely new appearance. The gap between each log was filled. All I had to do was fill the spaces between the stones with mortar. Pointing would ensure that each stone would stay in place and prevent cold winter winds from stealing the warmth from inside the cabin.

Everyone has a void in his or her heart that needs to be filled. I often tried to fill that void or yearning with the things of the world. As long as the flesh was satisfied, I could temporarily forget this void existed. Yet in times of idleness or when I became bored with the temporary fixes of the world, yearnings that something was missing began to resurface. The truth is the hole in my heart can only be permanently filled with the saving grace of my Lord and Savior Jesus Christ.

Prayer

Dear Heavenly Father, I am glad for the temporary pleasures
You allow me to experience as a human, but I am forever
grateful for my salvation in Christ Jesus. Amen.

JULY 2
DAY 183

"If your brother sins against you, go and show him
his fault, just between the two of you. If he listens
to you, you have won your brother over."
MATTHEW 18:15

Lyme Burning Open Wounds

It was time to start pointing. I opened my first of the six bags of Quikcrete that I needed to complete the job. I poured a quarter of the bag into my wheelbarrow. Then I took a bucket of water and added it to the gray powder. I used my hoe to mix the two ingredients together. When the consistency was just the way I wanted it, I was ready to start pointing. I took my trowel and slapped a mound of mud on my mortarboard. I was not able to use a pointing tool, so I used my fingers to push the mortar into the cracks between the stones. The week following I did not have to wonder what I did the previous weekend. The burning sensation I had in the smallest open wound on my hands from the industrial lyme in the mortar mix was a constant reminder.

There are times when I make the mistake of criticizing others when they sin. It is like pouring salt or industrial lyme onto an open wound. Instead of criticizing, I need to remember I too am a sinner and have been forgiven by a Heavenly Father who loves me.

Prayer

> *Dear Lord, use me to help my brothers and sisters in Christ walk closer with You and let me repent and not be offended when a fellow Christian reveals a sin in my life. Amen.*

JULY 3
DAY 184

And through him to reconcile to himself all things, whether things on earth or things in heaven, by making peace through his blood, shed on the cross.
COLOSSIANS 1:20

Using Protective Gloves

Using a pain scale of one to ten with ten being unbearable pain, the pain from the lyme in my open cuts was a six. I did not notice any soreness until the end of the day. Then once the pain started, I could not get it to stop even after washing my hands free of the lyme. Between the pain from the lyme in my cuts and my fingertips being tender from the abrasiveness of the mortar, I knew my hands were part of my body.

The following weekend I made sure to wear a protective glove on the hand I pointed with.

I am protected from God's judgment by the blood of Christ. The blood Jesus shed on the cross covers my sins. This is what makes it possible for me to have fellowship with my Heavenly Father. We are justified through the blood of Christ, just as if I had paid the penalty of death for my sins (Rom. 5:1).

Prayer

> *Thank You, Jesus, for taking my place on the cross. Let my obedience to You show the gratefulness I have for Your sacrifice. Amen.*

JULY 4
DAY 185

We do not want you to become lazy, but to imitate those who through faith and patience inherit what has been promised.
HEBREWS 6:12

Lazy Days of Summer

When it is ninety degrees and the humidity is high, the last thing I want to do is engage in some type of physical activity. These conditions, which are not uncommon throughout the summer, are more conducive to sedentary activities. Like sitting under a big shade tree with an ice-cold lemonade or sitting inside reading a good book with the air conditioning on, or possibly sitting in a mountain stream with the rush of cool water against your skin. I guess this is the reason we have the saying "the long lazy days of summer." But even though it is hot and humid, there are chores and responsibilities I need to complete.

God does not want me to become lackadaisical in my walk with Him. It will be at one of those unguarded moments when Satan will cause me to stumble. "Idle hands are the devil's workshop." I need to choose all of my activities carefully so as not to compromise my walk with God.

Prayer

> *Heavenly Father, help me to run my life with the perseverance needed to please You in all I do. Let me not become lazy or inattentive in my walk with You, especially during times of leisure. Amen.*

JULY 5
DAY 186

The weapons we fight with are not the weapons of the world. On the contrary, they have divine power to demolish strongholds.
2 CORINTHIANS 10:4

Breaking Loose a Big Rock

One of the more time-consuming jobs that needed to be done in building the log cabin was that of gathering mountain stone. I used mountain stone for chinking, for the fireplace, and for the floor. In most cases, the mountain stone was taken from a stone pile or from the top of the ground that could be loosened with a yank from my arm. However, there were times when I needed to pry the rock loose from the ground. In these situations, I used a digging iron and fulcrum to break the rock free from the stronghold the ground had on it.

Once I allow the thought of sin to take root in my mind, it does not take long for Satan to build a stronghold in my Christian walk. It is my desire to be vigilant and take the precautionary measures necessary to avoid Satan's tactics. I need to ask God to reveal any sin in my life and deal with it accordingly to break all strongholds Satan might have on me.

Prayer

> *Dear Heavenly Father, reveal to me any areas in my life that might provide Satan a place for building a stronghold. Let me be quick to confess sin and defeat Satan by examining each thought that enters my mind. Amen.*

JULY 6
DAY 187

*If a man cleanses himself from the latter, he will be
an instrument for noble purposes, made holy, useful to
the Master and prepared to do any good work.*
2 TIMOTHY 2:21

Mixing the Mortar

The key to pointing is having the mortar just right in consistency. If the mortar was too runny, you could not push it into the cracks, and if the mortar was too dry, it would just crumble and fall out. It does not take much water to go from a too dry condition to being too wet. I usually got my mortar mixture a little to runny then I would add small portions of Quickcrete until I had the mixture just right to be useful in pointing.

If I want to be useful to God, I need to have the ability to walk in the world but live in the Spirit. If I am too worldly, the unsaved will not see Jesus. The closer I walk to God the more in tune my heart will be with His and the more useful I will be in His hands.

Prayer

Dear Lord, let me be the right consistency in Your hands so that I am useful in sharing Your love with others. Amen.

JULY 7
DAY 188

He is before all things, and in him all things hold together.
COLOSSIANS 1:17

Holding the Stones Together

Pointing took as long as putting the stone in place. I could point one side in a day. With four sides to do, it would take me four Saturdays to have the job of pointing completed. My goal was to be done by the beginning of August. Most of the mountain stone I had in place was wedged tightly in place, but there were the exceptions. Pointing took care of that problem. After every nook and cranny was filled with mortar, each stone was held firmly in place.

I walk in faith not by sight. Faith is what holds me close to God. Faith is the mortar that strengthens my relationship with my Heavenly Father. I need to put my trust in God. Even if everything around me seems to be falling apart, I know if I hold on tightly to God, He will hold me firmly in His hands.

Prayer

Dear Heavenly Father, thank You for all Your blessings and for all answered prayers. Help my testimony remain in place so I can share with others Your faithfulness in my life. Amen.

JULY 8

DAY 189

My soul is weary with sorrow; strengthen me according to your word.
PSALM 119:28

Drying Time

Two hours after pointing a section of mountain stone, the mortar was stiff but not completely dry. It was at this stage of the mortar curing I would take a wire brush and clean off any excess mortar on the stones or logs. Once brushed, the pointing lines were more defined, and the different colors of mountain stone could be seen clearly. It usually took twenty-four hours for the mortar to completely dry. Once dry the mortar would turn a light gray and was as solid as the stones it was holding together.

The Bible is God's Word without error. I need to read God's Words daily to strengthen my walk with Him. It takes time for the Scriptures to solidify their influence on me so I am able to love others as God loves me.

Prayer

> *Heavenly Father, let me never grow weary of reading Your Word. I pray that as each day passes the Spirit will reveal new truths for me to hold on to so my relationship with You strengthens. Amen.*

JULY 9
DAY 190

Do not be hasty in the laying on of hands, and do not share in the sins of others. Keep yourself pure.
1 TIMOTHY 5:22

Boundaries

After the cabin was built, I had leftover sections of logs of various lengths. There was also some deadfall lying around that needed to be cleaned up. I decided to put these logs to use by laying them along the pathways and around the picnic area, forming a boundary. It would be easier to keep this area free of fallen limbs and larger stones sticking out of the ground. This way if I stay within the boundaries of the walkways and picnic area I am less likely to stumble.

I need to put up boundaries in my life also to keep me from stumbling into sin. Satan is a master at attacking areas of weakness in my life. When I know my weaknesses, it is best I set boundaries ahead of time to help me from even being tempted.

Prayer

> *Dear Heavenly Father, You know my faults. Reveal those areas in my life so I can set guidelines to follow to keep me in fellowship with You. Amen.*

JULY 10
Day 191

*Come, let us bow down in worship, let us
kneel before the LORD our Maker.*
Psalm 95:6

A Gathering Place

Within the bordered area, I have a bench, two vinyl chairs, and two small tables that sit around the fire ring and a picnic table that seats eight. Throughout the spring, summer, and fall it is a gathering place for family and friends. It is a place where we can be reenergized from our busy schedules by enjoying good food and conversation around the relaxing sound of a crackling fire.

God is pleased when believers gather to give Him praise and worship. Whether it is at church, at a home Bible study, or at campground meetings it is important for me to get into the habit of meeting with others to keep my spiritual fuel tank filled.

Prayer

Father, thank You for the freedom we enjoy in America to gather as Your church. Amen.

JULY 11
Day 192

*Let us rejoice and be glad and give him glory! For the wedding
of the Lamb has come, and his bride has made herself ready.*
Revelation 19:7

Family Reunion

Throughout America each year, usually during the months of summer, the tradition of having a family reunion is carried out. In most cases, it is an outdoor affair that takes place at a park with a pavilion. It is the one time of year when great-grandparents, grandparents, parents, children, uncles, aunts, cousins, nephews, and nieces all gather for a day of food and reminiscing.

When a person is spiritually born again they are born into the family of God (John 1:12). We are all brothers and sisters in Christ. The Bible speaks of a day when we will all gather for a great family reunion, when the bride of Christ, the church, will celebrate in heaven the wedding feast with the Lamb of God, Jesus Christ.

Prayer

> *Thank You, Heavenly Father, for the hope You give me each day as I look forward with expectation of the eternal family reunion I will have with You in heaven. Amen.*

JULY 12
DAY 193

Do not let any unwholesome talk come out of your mouths, but only what is helpful for building others up according to their needs, that it may benefit those who listen.
EPHESIANS 4:29

Uplifting Conversation

Picnics are a time for food and fun. Picnics are usually a gathering of people who know one another. Whether the group is made up of family, friends, fellow parishioners, or coworkers, there is a common thread that draws people together at a picnic. Conversations at picnics are generally uplifting and are filled with questions and answers on how things are going in the lives of one another since your last meeting.

It is God's desire that as brothers and sisters in Christ we uplift one another with our spoken words. When I speak, I want to edify the people who are listening. The saying "Think before you speak" is good for everyone to live by. Words can make or break someone's day.

Prayer

Heavenly Father, help me to control my tongue so the words that come out of my mouth would be a blessing to those who hear them. Amen.

JULY 13
DAY 194

And he took the children in his arms, put his hands on them and blessed them.
MARK 10:16

Picnics Are for Kids

For children picnics are one of the highlights of the summer. My family reunion was one of the biggest occasions I looked forward to each year. We played touch football, softball, and games for the kids, which included my favorite, the water balloon toss. The picnic was an all day affair. We would arrive by ten in the morning and get home after dark. Our reunion was beside a country club where a small stream separated the picnic grounds from the one fairway; of course, I always had to look for golf balls in the stream. I have fond memories of these picnics from my childhood.

Jesus loved the children and gave a harsh warning to anyone who would lead a child astray (Luke 17:1–3). I try my best to protect all children from the impurities in the world, so they too will have fond memories of their childhood.

Prayer

Dear Heavenly Father, help me to be a good witness to the children I encounter. Amen.

JULY 14
DAY 195

How much more will those who receive God's abundant provision of grace and of the gift of righteousness reign in life through the one man, Jesus Christ.
ROMANS 5:17

Abundance of Food

One thing always true of picnics I have been to is that there is always an abundance of food. At our family reunion, we had sweet corn done over an open fire. We would lay the corn on top of a metal plate covered with damp burlap bags until done. It was delicious. Picnics are not an occasion where you want to count calories. From all the meats done on the grill, potato salad, macaroni salad, chips, candy, cakes, pies, and soda pop to wash everything down, the calories are overflowing.

The period we live in is sometimes referred to as "the age of grace," meaning I live in a time when I can have my relationship with God restored. God's grace is overflowing and abundant; no matter what sin I have committed it would never be too great for God's grace not to cover. Grace is not deserved or something I can earn. No matter how many times I sin, God's grace will be sufficient to restore my relationship with Him.

Prayer

Heavenly Father, thank You for Your abundant grace, as John Newton wrote in his song "Amazing Grace": "Amazing grace, how sweet the sound / To save a wretch like me." Amen.

JULY 15

DAY 196

The wise, however, took oil in jars along with their lamps.
MATTHEW 25:4

Being Prepared

Preparation is the key to any good picnic. As a child I could not wait for picnics, they were synonymous with food, fun and games. Of course, I did not have to get too involved with all the preparation it takes to get ready for a picnic. Preparing the food and filling the ice chests, transporting everything to the chosen site, tending the grill, and clean up. Picnics are so much fun for children because as children we do not understand all the work and preparation it takes to have a good picnic.

Jesus wants me to be prepared when He comes for me. Whether through death or at the rapture of the church, I want to be prepared for my reunion with my Lord and Savior. Each day I should make every effort to be living more like Jesus.

Prayer

Heavenly Father, help me to live each moment for Your glory. Let me take captive every thought so I will be prepared and not ashamed when You come for me (1 John 2:28). Amen.

JULY 16

DAY 197

But the Lord said to Samuel, 'Do not consider his appearance or his height, for I have rejected him. The Lord does not look at the things man looks at. Man looks at the outward appearance, but the Lord looks at the heart.
1 SAMUEL 16:7

The Interior

Once I had the outside of the cabin done, it was time to work on the interior. In the years to come the appearance of the cabin on the outside will not change. The décor on the inside will change over the years. Different mementos will come and go, and with a bit of skill different hunting trophies will adorn the walls. The appearance on the inside will change with mementos left from visitors. The inside of the cabin will be a place for change to take place.

One of my favorite verses in the Bible is 1 Samuel 16:7. After I became an adult my appearance on the outside does not change drastically from year to year. However, once I accepted Jesus as my personal Savior my heart should be experiencing daily transformation. My attitudes and temperament should be becoming more like Christ each day.

Prayer

Dear Heavenly Father, help me not to be quick to judge someone by his or her outside appearance. I pray too that I continue to change from within to be more like Your Son, Jesus. Amen.

JULY 17
DAY 198

For everything that was written in the past was written
to teach us, so that through endurance and the encour-
agement of the Scriptures we might have hope.
ROMANS 15:4

Decorating with Memories from the Past

Where I am presently living is the fifth house I have lived in since
being married. In each case, my wife has a wonderful knack for
turning a house into a home with the way she decorates. We both like
country décor, so the more stuff hanging from the walls and things
lying on the floor, the better. I do not get involved with decorating the
house; however, the decorations of the cabin were all mine to decide. I
chose items that would be useful and would bring back good outdoor
memories.

I do not want to live in the past and constantly beat myself up for
things that could have, would have, or should have been. It is good,
though, that I learn from the past so I do not make the same mistakes
in the future.

Prayer

Heavenly Father, help me to use the past to remember all of the
times You were faithful in answering prayers and help me to
use the past to avoid sins made by others and myself. Amen.

JULY 18

DAY 199

*Multitudes, multitudes in the valley of decision! For the
day of the LORD is near in the valley of decision.*
JOEL 3:14

Decorating Decisions

It was time to decorate the cabin. The first things to go up on the walls were the four sets of antlers I had hanging out in the shed. I had to make decisions where the table and chairs were going, where to put the rocking chair and a place for all my cast iron cookware. Space was at a premium. I added shelves on the one wall to store a variety of items and mounted a cutting board on hinges that could be flipped up when not in use. I hung two gun racks up across from one another on either side of the wall. I was pleased with the look and practicality of my choices for décor after each item found its place.

In life, I am constantly making choices. What to eat, wear, and do and the words I speak are just a few of the things I decide daily. Every decision I make has a consequence. As I grow in Christ all of my decisions should be pleasing to God.

Prayer

Heavenly Father, reveal to me areas in my life where my daily choices need to be changed to walk closer to You. Help me with decisions I need to make through life to bring glory to You and bring others into Your kingdom. Amen.

JULY 19

DAY 200

*Keep your lives free from the love of money and be
content with what you have, because God has said,
'Never will I leave you; never will I forsake you'.*
HEBREWS 13:5

Rain or Shine

Once I started working on the interior, I felt a sigh of relief. Even
though there were a few obstacles to cross, like stripping the bark off
the logs, I knew I was going to be able to complete the cabin on time. It
did not matter if it was raining or not, the inside was leak proof thanks
to the galvanized tin roof. My progress would no longer be affected by
weather.

In life, I am going to experience successes and failures. There will be
times I am sad and times I will be glad. Each day brings new challenges
and an array of emotions. Whether I am going through a storm or the
skies of life are clear, I know God is by my side.

Prayer

*Thank you, Heavenly Father, for Your desire to fill my life
with joy. Let me trust in You knowing that You will never
forsake me. Amen.*

JULY 20

DAY 201

*For whoever keeps the whole law and yet stumbles at
just one point is guilty of breaking all of it.*
JAMES 2:10

Horseshoes (Close Is Okay)

Across from the path that leads up to the cabin, I put in horseshoe pits. I used three four-foot sections of logs to border the pits. I put a log in the back and one on each side. I had to remove as much mountain stone as I could, then I filled in the pits with dirt and pine needles. The horseshoes still have a tendency to bounce out of the pit if they do not land right; however, when throwing horseshoes getting close to the mark is okay.

Getting close might be okay for horseshoes, but getting to heaven demands perfection, which is impossible for man. The Bible tells me that all have sinned (Rom. 3:23). Thankfully, God loved me so much that He provided a way for me to have my sins removed. Jesus, the Son of God, left His heavenly dwelling place (Phil. 2:6–7) and lived a sinless life as a man on earth. He then paid the price for all men's sins by His crucifixion on the cross. When I received Jesus as my Savior, the blood He shed covered my sins; therefore, in God's eyes I am justified and have hit the mark of perfection.

Prayer

Thank You, Heavenly Father, for the wonderful power of the blood Your Son shed to cover the sins of those who believe in Him. Amen.

JULY 21
DAY 202

For prophecy never had its origin in the will of men, but men spoke from God as they were carried along by the Holy Spirit.
2 PETER 1:21

Cabin Journal

My least favorite subject in elementary school was English. Diagramming sentences was always a struggle for me. Some day I would enjoy taking a course in basic grammar. I never imagined I would enjoy writing as much as I do; I really enjoy the challenge of putting my thoughts on paper by choosing the right words and putting them in order to express myself clearly. I have to give my dad credit for the desire to write. He keeps a hunting journal and has always encouraged me to write down my experiences after a day's hunt.

God is not the author of confusion. Through spiritually inspired writings, He has documented the history of man from creation to my glorified body in heaven. He has given me a manual to live by. If I am obedient to His Word, my life will be full of joy.

Prayer

Heavenly Father, I am grateful for Your infallible Word. Let me never weary of reading the Bible. Continue to teach me through the Holy Spirit the truths in Your Holy Word. Amen.

JULY 22
DAY 203

Will you not revive us again, that your people may rejoice in you?
PSALM 85:6

Thunderstorms

I looked forward to summertime thunderstorms as a child growing up. No sooner would the storm pass than I would be outside dressed in shorts with no shoes splashing through every puddle I could find. The storms usually brought relief from the heat and humidity. I still enjoy thunderstorms today. They fill all your senses. You can smell the rain coming, feel the change in temperature see the lighting flash across the sky and listen to the thunder rumble. Thunderstorms have a way of reviving me to become more active.

I know there will be times in my life when I will face the physical and spiritual storms. It is during these times I find relief in God for He works all things for the good for those who love Him (Rom. 8:28).

I also need to pray for revival for those who do not know the peace of God. The world needs to hear the good news I have in Jesus Christ.

Prayer

Dear Heavenly Father, I pray for revival in our community, nation, and world. Amen.

JULY 23
DAY 204

The man who had received the five talents brought the other five. 'Master,' he said 'you entrusted me with five talents. See, I have gained five more.' "His master replied, 'Well done, good and faithful servant! You have been faithful with a few things.'"
MATTHEW 25:20–21

Sweat Equity

I remember my Dad saying, "Just because you are poor doesn't mean you have to be lazy." As I grew older, I took those words to heart. I am blessed with good physical health so I do not mind a long day of physical work, whether it is cutting and splitting wood or planting trees. Wherever Carol and I moved we would always keep up with the home maintenance. With me working on the outside and Carol taking care of the inside, our properties always looked better when we sold them than when we bought them. Most of these improvements could be credited to hard work with little or no financial aid. I call this sweat equity.

God wants me to use the way He created me for His glory. Whatever physical, mental, or spiritual attributes I have, God wants me to use all He has given me to fulfill the plan He has for my life.

Prayer

Heavenly Father, let me not be lackadaisical in using all the gifts and talents You have given me. Amen.

JULY 24

DAY 205

*"You are the salt of the earth. But if the salt loses its
saltiness, how can it be made salty again?"*
MATTHEW 5:13

Sunflower Seeds

Where we used to live, we had a swing with two benches facing one
another with a canopy over the top. When the neighbor boy saw us on
the swing, he would come over and talk with a mouthful of sunflower
seeds. This is how I was introduced to the art of eating sunflower seeds.
Now I can put a handful of sunflower seeds into my mouth and skill-
fully remove the shell from the seed with my front teeth, spit out the
shell and eat the seed before I start on the next one. When I worked
on the cabin in summer and the sweat was rolling off my brow, eating
sunflower seeds was a good way to replenish the salts in my body.

Salt has many beneficial properties. It is good for curing meat,
adding flavor to foods, cleaning wounds, and keeping someone from
getting muscle cramps. However, once salt loses its saltiness it has no
value. This is why Jesus tells me to be the salt of the world. People who
do not know Jesus should be able to see a difference in the way I live
my life. I too have to be careful not to lose my saltiness and become
useless for God's work.

Prayer

*Dear Heavenly Father, I pray that You use my life to season
or cure the lives of people in a world without the hope of Jesus.
Amen.*

JULY 25
DAY 206

*I am not saying this because I am in need, for I have
learned to be content whatever the circumstances.*
PHILIPPIANS 4:11

Mortar (Only Make What You Can Use)

When I mixed my mortar for pointing the mountain stone, I had to
be careful not to make too much. If I made too much it would begin to
dry out and crumble into pieces before I was able to use all of it. After
some trial and error, I got good at measuring out just what I needed so
none of the cement would go to waste. I usually made it a little on the
wet side to give me a little more time before it dried out. The key was
only to make enough that I could use.

God wants me to be content with what I have. Whether in times
of plenty or in times of little, I must put my trust in God for I know
His grace is sufficient for me. God's Word tells me not to be envious or
worry what others have (Ps. 37:7).

Prayer

*Thank You, Heavenly Father, for the countless blessings I have
in my life. Help me to be grateful and content with each breath
You give me. Amen.*

JULY 26
DAY 207

*And he went and lived in a town called Nazareth. So was fulfilled
what was said through the prophets: 'He was called a Nazarene.'*
MATTHEW 2:23

Flatlanders

Carol and I were both raised in Lancaster County. Lancaster County is best known for its population of Amish. The Amish farms, shops, and cuisine draw tourists from all over the world.

Carol and I lived in the city of Lancaster for seven years when we decided to move back to the country. Our prayers were answered when we bought the home we now live in, in the small mountain community of Shunk in Sullivan County, Pennsylvania. We are transplants better known as flatlanders. Once a flatlander, always a flatlander. You might be a flatlander if one of the things you truly miss is having a pizza delivered to your house.

We have all heard the saying "Stick and stones can break your bones but names can never hurt you." Jesus had names associated with Him for where He lived. He was born in the small community of Bethlehem where it was said that nothing good could possibly come from there. He later moved to Nazareth where He was known as a Nazarene for the way He dressed and kept His hair.

Prayer

> *Heavenly Father, help me never to be judgmental of someone's cultural status, birthplace, or upbringing. Let me be a reflection of Jesus to everyone I encounter. Amen.*

JULY 27
DAY 208

In my Father's house are many rooms; if it were not so, I would have told you. I am going there to prepare a place for you.
JOHN 14:2

Preparing the Interior

It took several weekends to get the interior of the cabin completed. When doing the interior I had several things in mind. One being practicality: I hung camping tools, added shelves and hooks for storage; another being pleasure: I decorated with pieces of memorabilia that brought back pleasant thoughts of the past; and another being comfort: I wanted to rough it as comfortably as possible.

It took God seven days to create the heavens and earth. I once had a pastor who made the comment, "Can you imagine what heaven will look like if He has been working on it for an eternity?" I can only imagine the beauty of heaven. I can be reassured when I think the One who died for me and had victory over death is preparing a dwelling place especially for me when I pass through the doorway of death.

Prayer

Heavenly Father, I am grateful for the hope I have in spending an eternity with You in heaven. Amen.

JULY 28
DAY 209

For though I am absent from you in body, I am present with you in spirit and delight to see how orderly you are and how firm your faith in Christ is.
COLOSSIANS 2:5

Shelves, Hooks, and Gun Racks

With the cabin only having an inside dimension of ten feet by nine feet, there was no room for clutter. I have ninety square feet of floor space, and sixty square feet of loft space. Everything had to have a place and there needed to be a place for everything. I accomplished this by using shelves, hooks and gun racks. If everything is done in an orderly manner, there is enough room for two people and gear to hunt or camp comfortably.

There have been a number of times when I have heard someone say they do not read the Bible because it is too confusing. God is not the author of confusion. When God created the heavens and the earth, He did so in an orderly manner. He desires for me to live my Christian life in an orderly manner. My physical body needs sleep and food and my spiritual body needs to spend time with God. An orderly life is a happy life.

Prayer

> *Heavenly Father, in a world where there is so much confusion, help me to maintain peace and order in my life. Amen.*

JULY 29
DAY 210

Now Elijah the Tishbite, from Tishbe in Gilead, said to Ahab, "As the Lord, the God of Israel, lives, whom I serve, there will be neither dew or rain in the next few years except at my word."
1 KINGS 17:1

Draught

We moved to Shunk on September 15, 1999. The following summer we had a drought. Farmers lost fields of corns, mountain streams that flow year round dried up, and "no burn" ordinances were put into effect. Everyone's lawns were brown. I did not have to mow grass from June until August. It even brought up conversations of the dust bowls out west in the early 1900s. Without water, plants stop growing and eventually die.

The same is true for my Christian walk. After I accepted Jesus as my personal Savior, my newfound faith needed to be watered spiritually for me to grow. I know I will experience spiritual droughts in my life. This is why I attend church regularly and have daily devotions. It does not take long for my spiritual tank to be drained from the world I live in.

Prayer

> *Dear Heavenly Father, I pray my spiritual vessel stays full so I will be an effective witness for You and grow spiritually in a way that would be pleasing to You. Amen.*

JULY 30
DAY 211

*And you also were included in Christ when you heard the word
of truth, the gospel of your salvation. Having believed, you
were marked in him with a seal, the promised Holy Spirit.*
EPHESIANS 1:13

Tin Cans and Coolers

I needed containers to keep camping supplies dry and critter proof.
Knowing this, my wife, who is the queen of yard sales, bought me
several tin cans with outdoor scenes on them. These cans really proved
useful in keeping all sorts of items organized and safe. I also have two
coolers I use, one to keep cookware and utensils together and the other
cooler I use to keep cooking ingredients dry, such as, flour, sugar, salt,
seasonings, cornmeal and brown sugar. The tin can and coolers proved
to be invaluable for keeping supplies sealed.

When I accepted Jesus as my Savior, my inheritance of heaven was
guaranteed. I am sealed by the Holy Spirit. Nothing can penetrate the
salvation I have in Christ Jesus.

Prayer

*Thank You, Heavenly Father, for Your assured hope of salva-
tion and the assurance of having the Holy Spirit. Amen.*

JULY 31
DAY 212

*In the same way, faith by itself, if it is not
accompanied by action, is dead.*
JAMES 2:17

Stagnate Water

Water needs to move to remain healthy. Even lakes and ponds have inlets and outlets to keep the water replenished. One precaution to curb the spread of the West Nile virus is to get rid of all pools of standing water, which are breeding grounds for mosquitoes. A pool of water without any movement will become stagnate. It will begin to smell bad and will be unsuitable for consumption.

In my Christian walk, I need to keep moving forward. I have to keep growing spiritually. If I remain idle, I too will become useless to God, like stagnate water is to man. It is my goal to become a little more Christlike with each passing day.

Prayer

Heavenly Father, help me to grow spiritually. When I reach plateaus of growth in my Christian walk, show me the way to keep moving forward in my walk with You. Amen.

AUGUST 1
Day 213

And no wonder, for Satan himself masquerades as an angel of light.
2 Corinthians 11:4

Invisible Destruction

For the next week, I am going to be writing about bore worms. If I had known beforehand what problems this inch-long grub could cause, I would have done things differently. I had heard of such creatures but for some reason I felt my cabin would not be susceptible to their infestation. As I was building the cabin, there was no evidence the logs had bore worms. However, as I was soon to learn, just because you do not see them does not mean they are not there.

Satan is for real. Just because I do not see him does not mean he is not there. The Bible makes mention of him from Genesis to the book of Revelation. He would like me to think he is fictitious. The truth is his message has not changed from the day he caused Adam and Eve to rebel against God. It is his desire for me to believe that I can live without God. He wants me to fulfill the desires of the flesh so I will join him in his fallen state from God.

Prayer

Dear Heavenly Father, I pray that You will protect me from the evil one. Let me be quick to resist temptations. Amen.

AUGUST 2
Day 214

Say to the Israelites: 'When a man or woman wrongs another in any way and so is unfaithful to the LORD, that person is guilty and must confess the sin he has committed."
Numbers 5:6–7

Big Problem if Left Alone

Most of the bore worms that I saw were no bigger than an inch long. I do not know how far they can burrow in a day but for a creature so small, the channels in the wood were quite impressive. I could easily imagine the damage capable of being done by thousands of beetle larvae. Like any wood-destroying insect such as the carpenter bee or termite, if left alone they can cause irreversible problems.

Sin is much the same way in a person's life. Sin often starts out very small but if left unconfessed it will eventually turn into a habit or lead to other sins to cover up the original sin. The story of David and Bathsheba (2 Sam. 11:1–12:14) is a perfect example of the latter. For every action, there is a reaction, and for every sin, there is a consequence. I can minimize the consequences of sin if I confess my sins immediately with a sincere heart of repentance.

Prayer

Dear Lord, I pray that You will continually reveal to me sin in my life so I can be quick to repent so sin will not destroy my relationship with You. Amen.

AUGUST 3
DAY 215

For since the creation of the world God's invisible qualities—his eternal power and divine nature—have been clearly seen, being understood from what has been made, so that men are without excuse.
ROMANS 1:20

Sawdust Mounds

When I first saw the little mounds of sawdust, I was not very concerned. I had so much sawdust and woodchips lying around, I thought it might be a product of something I did. It did not take long to differentiate between the two. The little mounds of dirt began appearing on every log. I would sweep the mounds away only to see them return the next day. The mounds were two inches wide and an inch high. When I swept them all together, I would dispose of it by the shovelfuls. There was no denying I had a problem.

God tells me in the first chapter of Romans that man is without an excuse in believing there is no God. Since the beginning of creation,

God's visible evidence of His existence has been on full display for man to see.

Prayer

> *Dear Heavenly Father, thank You for giving me Your Holy Word. Your creation and Your intervention in my life leave me without a doubt that You are in control of all things. Amen.*

AUGUST 4
DAY 216

For Ezra had devoted himself to the study and observance of the Law of the LORD, and to teaching its decrees and laws in Israel.
EZRA 7:10

Researching Bore Worms

Once I realized I had a problem, I had to find out what was causing the mounds of sawdust to appear. I started by peeling the bark from the logs. It did not take long for me to come face to face with nasty-looking, segmented, grub-like creatures. They were no longer than an inch, a little thicker than baling twine, and cream colored with a brown head. What was I looking at? More importantly, how could I get rid of them? After asking several people in the area who work with wood, I came to find out that I was looking at the larvae of a wood beetle and they needed to be sprayed with a pesticide.

I cannot take care of a problem until I know what it is. Satan and his demons try their best to cause problems for me as I try to live a Christian life. Jesus gives a perfect example on how to deal with this problem when He was tempted by Satan in the fourth chapter of Luke. The better I know God's Word the easier it will be to fight off the devil's attacks.

Prayer

> *Heavenly Father, thank You for your written Word. Give me the desire to keep Your Word in my heart and give me the*

ability to remember Your truths when tempted by the evil one. Amen.

AUGUST 5
DAY 217

"Now leave me alone so that my anger may burn against them and that I may destroy them. Then I will make you into a great nation."
EXODUS 32:10

Destroy the Cabin

Every day I swept away mounds of wood dust left behind from the destructive work of the bore worms. Not only were there mounds of wood dust, but you could actually hear the bore worms at work. The sound they made was similar to rubbing two pieces of sandpaper against one another. Imagine several hundred worms at work making this noise. To me it sounded like an army of loggers clearing out a rain forest. All I could picture was walking up to my cabin and it being a pile of wood dust. The thought crossed my mind to burn down the cabin so I wouldn't have to listen to the continuous noise and slow destruction.

That thought opened my eyes to how my Heavenly Father must feel when humanity repeatedly rises up against Him. His beloved chosen people were continually rebelling, even after their miraculous deliverance from the Pharaoh. God destroyed the world once by the flood and He thought of destroying His chosen people after they worshiped the golden calf.

Prayer

Heavenly Father, You have shown great patience with me as I grow in my Christian faith. Help me to show the same patience to others in the process of walking with You or those who do not know You. Amen.

AUGUST 6
DAY 218

I urge you, brothers, to watch out for those who cause divisions and put obstacles in your way that are contrary to the teaching you have learned. Keep away from them.
ROMANS 16:17

Infecting the Living Trees

Not only were there little mounds of wood dust all over the cabin, they were all over the logs that lined my paths and picnic ground area. It seemed like the wood beetles were infecting every log that was cut. I read that they are attracted by the smell of pinesap. That could easily explain the reason for the infestation. My greatest fear was the possibility of the wood beetle infecting the living trees. All I could imagine was my beautiful stand of pines dying from the destructive work of the bore worms.

One of the greatest fears of a pastor is the infiltration of Satan and his destructive work in the hearts of his congregation. There are many verses from the apostles warning the early church of false prophets and teachers. Satan is constantly striving to cause disharmony and division within the church.

Prayer

Dear Heavenly Father, I pray for the church daily and for the pastors to protect their sheep from Satan's infestation. Amen.

AUGUST 7
DAY 219

*"I will give you every place where you set
your foot, as I promised Moses."*
JOSHUA 1:3

Bore Worm Tracks

There was a hole in the bark the bore worm used to push out the
wood dust forming small mounds. Just like the person who tunnels from
one spot to the next needs to get rid of the dirt out of the hole where
they started. When I removed the bark to find the culprits responsible
for the wood dust piles, I could easily see the tracks left behind by the
bore worms. Long winding grooves in the wood lead me to my first
encounter to the bore worm.

I love the poem "Footprints in the Sand." It is a poem about footprints left behind as you walk in the sand. They go from two sets of
footprints to one set. It is when the footprints go to one set when the
author feels Jesus has stopped walking with her. In reality, it was when
Jesus was carrying her through the rough times in her life.

Prayer

*Jesus, it brings me great joy to know You are always with me.
I pray that the tracks I leave behind will lead others straight
to You. Amen.*

AUGUST 8
DAY 220

*And we know that in all things God works for the good of those
who love him, who have been called according to his purpose.*
ROMANS 8:28

Fears to Cheers

After the fleeting thoughts of destroying the cabin by fire subsided, I set my mind on what needed to be done. The bore worms actually turned out to be helpful in two ways. First, they loosened up the bark for removal. Their exit holes proved to be a good starting spot for removing the bark. Secondly, after the bark was removed from the entire log, the markings on the wood left behind from the tunneling the bore worms turned out to be quite creative.

The Christian life is not always going to be easy. There were and will be many times in life when I will face trials and tribulation. I can rest assured that even through the bad times, if I am in fellowship with God, He is in control. Even though I may not have the answers for the trials I am experiencing, God has promised me if I love Him, He will work all things for the good.

Prayer

> *Heavenly Father, as I go through trials in my life, give me the patience to wait for Your answers, and let me be submissive to Your will for my life, knowing that You love me and only want the best for me. Amen.*

AUGUST 9
DAY 221

My eyes are on all their ways; they are not hidden from me, nor is their sin concealed from my eyes.
JEREMIAH 16:17

Debarking Every Log

I could not actually see the bore worms by just looking at the cabin. I could see the consequences of their presence. The bore worms were hidden behind the bark and in some cases, they bored into the log. I needed to debark every log to reveal the infestation of the cabin. I took great pleasure in killing bore worms I uncovered as I peeled away their shield.

Sin is a lot like those bore worms. Other people can see the consequences of sin in a person's life. People like to keep their sins hidden from the ones they love. In some cases people are not even aware of the sins they are committing. Through family, friends or the Holy Spirit, sins need to be revealed to the sinner so they can take the steps necessary to destroy the sin in their life.

Prayer

Heavenly Father, reveal in me any areas in my life not pleasing to You. When revealed, let me deal with them quickly through repentance. Amen.

AUGUST 10
DAY 222

Who can discern his errors? Forgive my hidden faults. Keep your servant also from willful sins; may they not rule over me.
PSALM 19:12-13

Making Mistakes

I made two mistakes when I built the log cabin. The first one was not having the ridgepole extend two feet off the backside and the second mistake was not debarking the logs beforehand. Truth be told, I should have cut my logs, let them sit for a year, then remove the bark before starting my construction. The logs would have been lighter and easier to handle from the loss of bark and water weight. Fortunately, I was able to make things right through some innovative thinking and hard work.

After becoming a Christian one thing guaranteed to remain true is the fact I am going to make mistakes or sin. When I do, I simply need to make things right with God. I do that by asking for forgiveness and working hard not to make the same mistake when faced with a similar situation.

Prayer

Thank You, Heavenly Father, for Your forgiveness. I am grateful for Your patience with me as I work towards being more like Your Son. Amen.

AUGUST 11
DAY 223

"'If you can'?" said Jesus. "Everything is possible for him who believes."
MARK 9:23

Mission Impossible

I knew that eventually the bark on the logs would have to come off. I just did not foresee that eventually meant now. Somehow, I convinced myself that I could wait a year or two before tackling the bark-removing project. When my mind finally comprehended the task, it seemed like mission impossible. Some of the logs had only been cut a couple of months earlier and the bark was still tightly adhered to the wood. Fortunately, I was a month ahead of schedule and the bore worms sped up the natural process of loosening up the bark.

I enjoy reading biographies of missionaries, such as Hudson Taylor, Amy Carmichael, Gladys Aylward, and Bruce Olson to name a few. There were so many times when they were faced with an impossible situation. However, through their faith and prayers, what seemed humanly impossible was proven possible with God.

Prayer

Heavenly Father, I am grateful that I serve an all-powerful God. Help my faith grow by letting me stand to the side so that You can reveal Your power to me. Amen.

AUGUST 12
DAY 224

"Come, follow me," Jesus said, "and I will make you fishers of men."
MARK 1:17

Find the Right Tool

I felt the task of removing the bark was overwhelming, because the tools I used were not working very efficiently. I tried peeling the bark with knives, chisels, putty knives and screw drives. One day I tried my machete. The long thin sharp blade helped me remove large sections of bark in a single pass. It seemed to me the machete was made specifically for this job.

God wants me to be fishers of men. To catch men for Jesus I need to find the right tool. As a missionary for Christ, I have to get out of my comfort zone. I might have to adapt to customs of foreign people, like eating foods I do not like or even learning new languages to be the correct tool God can use to reach the lost.

Prayer

Dear Heavenly Father, help me to be the right instrument, to help others see their need to remove the sin in their lives and have a relationship with You. Amen.

AUGUST 13
DAY 225

But if we hope for what we do not yet have, we wait for it patiently.
ROMANS 8:25

Expectancy of Fall

August is the last full month of summer. Traditionally some of our hottest days come in the month of August. This is the time of year

I hear comments like; I cannot wait for fall to get here, when only five months earlier people were looking forward to the warmer weather. Personally, I look forward to the fall season with great expectancy. I enjoy being warmed by a fire as the temperatures begin to drop and seeing the fall colors on a sunlight mountainside.

As a Christian I have the pleasure of living each day with great expectancy. On any given day, the Lord of Lords might come back and rapture His bride into heaven, or on any given day, my Heavenly Father might ask me to walk through the doorway of death to see the glory of my personal Savior face to face.

Prayer

> *Thank You, Heavenly Father, for the anticipation I have of spending eternity with You in heaven, void of sin. Amen.*

AUGUST 14
DAY 226

I the LORD do not change. So you, O descen-
dants of Jacob, are not destroyed.
MALACHI 3:6

No Change at Camp

The chores I do during the summer months change each day. One night I will push mow, the next I will get on the riding mower, and the third night I will trim with the weed whacker. In between these chores there are the projects I need to finish before winter and the honey-do-list that never seems to end. Then before I know it, I have to start mowing again. I guess that is why I like the surroundings around the cabin so much. They do not change from season to season. There is no grass to cut, weeds to pull and the pines remain green all year.

I am grateful my God does not change. He is the same today as He was yesterday and as He will be tomorrow. His love is never ending. I do not ever need an appointment to meet with Him. He is always ready to hear from me.

Prayer

> *Thank You, Heavenly Father, for not changing like the wind.*
> *I rest securely knowing that You will be faithful in doing all*
> *You have said. Amen.*

AUGUST 15
DAY 227

Trust in the Lord with all your heart and lean
not on your own understanding.
PROVERBS 3:5

Unexpected Expenses

Debarking the whole cabin and killing all the bore worms that I saw was a start in the extermination process. The price for debarking was free; however, further measures of bug prevention would cost some money. These expenditures were unexpected. I bought a gallon of copper brown to treat the outside of the logs, pesticides specifically for bore worms, and a gallon of polyurethane to coat the logs inside the cabin.

There will be many times in life when I am going to be faced with unexpected situations. When the unforeseen occurs, I need to put my complete trust in God to see me through to the other side. It is during these times that help my trust in God will grow.

Prayer

> *Heavenly Father, I pray that I never lean on my own under-*
> *standing but always put my complete confidence in You in all*
> *I do in my life. Amen.*

AUGUST 16
DAY 228

*And we also thank God continually because, when you
received the word of God, which you heard from us, you
accepted it not as the word of men, but as it actually is, the
word of God, which is at work in you who believe.*
1 THESSALONIANS 2:13

Be Effective

After determining what pest control spray would be most effective, I
purchased a one-gallon container. I did not want to take any chances so
I went with a brand name in lieu of trying some generic product. The
container was fitted with an automatic pump for spraying with batteries
included. In order for the insecticide to be effective, I had to spray it on
the logs. It would be of no use if I just kept it in the plastic container.

When I accepted Jesus as my personal Savior, I was filled with the
Holy Spirit and Jesus comes to live in my heart. In God's eyes, I am
now a clean vessel He can use for His glory. I will not be effective if
I keep the Good News to myself. I need to share the gospel to those
around me.

Prayer

*Dear Heavenly Father, use me for Your glory. Help me to take
advantage of every opportunity You give me to share the love
that I have within me to those who have not heard the Good
News. Amen.*

AUGUST 17
DAY 229

But Moses said to God, "Who am I, that I should go to Pharaoh and bring the Israelites out of Egypt?" And God said, "I will be with you."
EXODUS 2:11–12

Uncomfortable Positions

It was very difficult to remove the bark from the crossbeams and trusses. Even with safety glasses, I got bark and dirt in my eyes from having to look up while debarking. The thinner logs made it harder to get large strips off at a time, also having to bend as if a pretzel to get to some of the places on the trusses made it an uncomfortable experience.

Moses did not feel comfortable when God asked him to lead his people out of Egypt. There are times when I feel uncomfortable or inadequate with what God wants me to do. I need to overcome these feelings for God to complete His will for me.

Prayer

Heavenly Father, I pray my feelings would not interfere with the work You desire to accomplish in my life. Amen.

AUGUST 18
DAY 230

Instead, it should be that of your inner self, the unfading beauty of a gentle and quiet spirit, which is of great worth in God's sight.
1 PETER 3:4

The Beauty Within

I enjoy working with wood. I get pleasure in the smell, the feel, and looking at the designs the grain makes in the wood. This is the reason the bark removing process was not as laborious for me as it might have been for someone else. As I removed the bark, it released the scent of pine into the air. The logs were no longer rough but smooth and now you could see the grain and the knots in the wood. Removing the bark revealed the beauty within.

I am sure we have all heard the saying "You can't judge a book by its cover." I cannot judge a person or discern their spiritual condition simply by looking at them. Christians come in all shapes and sizes. God made me just the way He wants me to look. He is much more interested in me getting my heart right with Him and striving to perfect my inner beauty.

Prayer

Dear Heavenly Father, help me not to be quick to judge appearances. Rather let me find the beauty within a person as I work on trying to reflect Jesus to others. Amen.

AUGUST 19
DAY 231

Do your best to present yourself to God as one approved, a workman who does not need to be ashamed and who correctly handles the word of truth.
2 TIMOTHY 2:15

Read All the Directions

The first thing I did when I got my insecticide home was to read the directions. The spray was pre-mixed so I did not have to worry about getting the solution correct. I still needed to know how the sprayer worked, when to spray, how much to spray and how many applications were needed for the best results. I always read the directions whenever I get something from the store I have not used before or needs to be put together. I need to read the directions so the product will be used safely and properly.

God's Word is much the same. God does not want me to select verses to fit my lifestyle. Doing this would be harmful in my relationship with God. I need to read the entire Bible in order to live my life correctly.

Prayer

Heavenly Father, I pray that the Holy Spirit will illuminate my mind so that I can apply Your word to my daily life in a such a way that I fulfill the plan You have for me. Amen.

AUGUST 20
DAY 232

Listen to advice and accept instruction, and in the end you will be wise.
PROVERBS 19:20

Use Copper Brown

After I treated the cabin with insecticide, I was ready to apply the Copper Brown. Copper Brown is the wood preservative that replaced creosote. I found out about Copper Brown from a friend at church. From experience, he told me that Copper Brown is an effective wood preserver as well as a deterrent to wood-infecting insects. His good advice helped save the cabin and my sanity.

Proverbs tells me that if I listen to good advice I will become wise. It is impossible for me to be an expert in everything. There are many times in life I need to ask the advice of others who have been through similar situations for me to make the correct decision.

Prayer

Dear Lord, let me not be prideful when I need the help of others to make a choice on how to deal with something I have never dealt with before and do not understand. Amen.

AUGUST 21
DAY 233

My son, do not despise the LORD's discipline and do resent his rebuke.
PROVERBS 3:11

Unpleasant Smell

I enjoy the sense of smell. Some of my favorite aromas are fresh ground coffee, sizzling bacon, onions frying in butter, the smell of fresh fall air, and honeysuckle. I truly do enjoy the olfactory organs. There are of course smells on the other side of the spectrum that are not so pleasant. Copper Brown falls into the unpleasant category. I needed to endure its bad odor to preserve the exterior logs of the cabin.

Being disciplined by God is a true sign that He loves me. Even though the experience may be unpleasant at the time, I understand God is trying to teach me a lesson. God will discipline me for my sins so in the future I will remember not to make the same mistakes.

Prayer

Dear Heavenly Father, help me to recognize Your discipline as an act of love to help me be a better person. Amen.

AUGUST 22
DAY 234

Three times I pleaded with the Lord to take it away from me. But he said to me, "My grace is sufficient for you, for my power is made perfect in weakness."
2 CORINTHIANS 12:8–9

Harsh but Beautifies

I wore latex gloves when I applied the Copper Brown. I did not want to have any bad experiences with skin irritation like the one I did when I used the mortar for pointing the mountain stone. Even though some of the products I used were harsh to the skin, they were necessary. The Copper Brown, as the name implies, stained the wood brown. In contrast with the light mountain stone and mortar, it truly enhanced the appearance of the cabin.

Sometimes God uses tragedy to bring forth beautiful testimonies. I vividly remember the testimony of a veteran whose face was completely burned from a bomb explosion while serving in Vietnam. His testimony for God brought me to tears. His love for the Heavenly Father and his sincerity in serving Him completely overshadowed his appearance. All I saw was his love for God and what He did for him.

Prayer

Heavenly Father, I pray that when the harshness of life comes my way I will come through it in a way that will bring glory to You. Amen.

AUGUST 23
DAY 235

As you know, we consider blessed those who have persevered. You have heard of Job's perseverance and have seen what the Lord finally brought about. The Lord is full of compassion and mercy.
JAMES 5:11

Preservative

After applying the Copper Brown to the outside of the cabin and realizing the smell associated with this product, I decided to preserve the wood on the inside with polyurethane. Though there is an initial odor with polyurethane, it does not linger like Copper Brown. Polyurethane is usually used as a protective top coat after staining. In this case, I just wanted to take advantage of its preservative qualities. I did not want to change the natural color of the wood on the inside of the cabin.

A preservative protects an object from natural deterioration. God wants me to persist in my Christian walk. He does not want me to deteriorate back to my old self. Perseverance is a quality I strive for. If I do not persevere, I will not know what God's blessing would have been for me.

Prayer

> *Dear Heavenly Father, I pray that I will persevere in my walk with You. Let me be steadfast in avoiding the temptation of the world. Amen.*

AUGUST 24
DAY 236

Therefore, my dear brothers, stand firm. Let nothing move you. Always give yourselves fully to the work of the Lord, because you know that your labor in the Lord is not in vain.
1 CORINTHIANS 15:58

Can't See the Difference

Polyurethane is clear. Its consistency is just a little thicker than water. When applying the polyurethane on the logs inside the cabin I had to be careful to make sure that I knew where I started and stopped. Except for a slightly glossier appearance, it was hard to distinguish between the treated and non-treated logs, especially with the poor lighting inside the cabin. After all the hard work of painting the inside was done, I really scarcely saw a difference

There are missionaries who labor a lifetime without ever seeing any results. Christians have gone to their graves before lifelong prayers have been answered. Sunday school teachers and youth group leaders who work with our young do not always see the fruits of their labor. There will be many times in my Christian walk when I want to see a difference from my effort for the Lord; however, I can rest assured as God has promised my labor will not be in vain.

Prayer

> *Heavenly Father, help me not to become discouraged when I do*
> *not see results for my prayers or ministries for you. Rather, let*
> *me press on and leave the results in your hands. Amen.*

AUGUST 25
DAY 237

If anyone does not provide for his relatives, and espe-
cially for his immediate family, he has denied the
faith and is worse than an unbeliever.
1 TIMOTHY 5:8

Taking Time to Pick Huckleberries

Sullivan County is blessed with beautiful mountain scenery, pris-
tine trout streams, sawmills and acres of huckleberry bushes. Every year
towards the end of July or the early part of August, the huckleberries
are ready to be picked. Huckleberries are wild blueberries. They are a
little smaller than their domestic counterparts, but to me taste just as
good. I always take the time each year to pick several quarts of the juicy,
sweet fruit.

As important as my job, church, and hobbies may be, it is vital that
I take the time to show my family how much I love them. I never heard
anyone say I wish I had spent more time at work. I have heard people,
including religious leaders, say, "I wish I would have spent more time
with my family."

Prayer

> *Dear Heavenly Father, besides the time I spend with You, let*
> *my family time be second most important in my life. Amen.*

AUGUST 26
DAY 238

Whatever you do, work at it with all your heart,
as working for the Lord, not for men.
COLOSSIANS 3:23

Learn to Say No

My priorities in life starting with most important are: God, family, work, church, and hobbies. With those five activities plus six hours of sleep a night, my days are usually filled. When I first became a Christian, I used to say yes to every opportunity that was offered me. It did not take long for all those yes's to become overwhelming. Once again, the wisdom of my loving wife taught me, though it took some time, it is okay to say no.

God wants me to do my best in all I do. If I say yes to every opportunity, one of the obligations will eventually suffer, because I am spreading myself to thin.

Prayer

Heavenly Father give me the wisdom to know the activities
You want me to be involved in so I can do all things to the best
of my ability for You. Amen.

AUGUST 27
DAY 239

If I am to go on living in the body, this
will mean fruitful labor for me.
PHILIPPIANS 1:22

Picking Huckleberries Is Work

When you first start filling your bucket up, it seems like it takes forever to get the bottom of the bucket covered. It usually takes an hour or more to pick three quarts of huckleberries. It is a tedious job picking those berries one at a time. The weather is still warm and the mosquitoes and bees can usually be heard and sometimes felt during berry picking time. Some of the best berries are toward the inside of the bushes so you have to make an extra effort to get to those chosen fruits.

One way you can tell a Christian apart from others is simply by witnessing the fruits of their labor. God wants me to labor in my earthly body for Him as I try to win souls for Him (Prov. 11:30).

Prayer

> *Heavenly Father, let me be tireless in my labor for You as I grow in my spiritual walk with You. Amen.*

AUGUST 28
DAY 240

Be self-controlled and alert. Your enemy the devil prowls around like a roaring lion looking for someone to devour.
1 PETER 5:8

Devoured by the Bear

Statistics will show you that there has never been anyone killed by a black bear in Sullivan County. Therefore, for my way of thinking, that makes the percentages even higher for there to be a first time. From May until August, we usually see a bear or the evidence of a bear visiting our home once a week. In big blueberry patches, you can see where the bears have broken the limbs on the bushes from dining on the luscious berries. I am not afraid of the bears but I do make a lot of noise so I do not surprise a mama bear and get in between her and her cubs. I do not want to be the first person to be devoured by a bear.

There is something far more dangerous than the bear I need to be concerned about, and that is Satan himself. He is relentless in his pursuit of looking for someone to devour. He is forever looking for ways to render me ineffective in my work for the Lord. He wants to ruin my witness so I do not bring others to the saving knowledge of Jesus Christ.

Prayer

Dear Heavenly Father, I pray that the spiritual armor in which I dress myself daily will protect me from the wiles of Satan and his demons. Amen.

AUGUST 29
DAY 241

"Let both grow together until the harvest. At that time I will tell the harvesters: 'First collect the weeds and tie them in bundles to be burned; then gather the wheat and bring it into my barn.'"
MATTHEW 13:30

Cleaning the Good from the Bad

Whenever I go to pick huckleberries the last instructions I hear from my wife before I walk out the door is to pick clean. I always start out with good intentions, picking one berry at a time, making sure it is at its peak of ripeness. It makes me feel like Juan Valdez picking only the best coffee beans. As hard as I try, I always end up with dry leaves and twigs in my bucket of huckleberries. This being the case, Carol usually ends up with the tedious job of separating the good berries from the debris.

It is not God's desire that any should perish, however there is going to come a time when God separates the wheat from the chaff, the goats from the lambs or the unrighteous from the righteous. When it comes to harvest time, I want to be included with the wheat.

Prayer

Dear Lord, help me to bring others to You so that on the Day of Judgment they will be included with the righteous. Amen.

AUGUST 30

Day 242

Rejoice and be glad, because great is your reward in heaven, for in the same way they persecuted the prophets who were before you.
Matthew 5:12

Tedious but Rewarding

When I was a child, I remember how I used to dread the times my dad would ask me to pick vegetables from the garden. As a child, all I saw was the work, and I was not very fond of them when they were served for supper. As an adult, I take on a completely new perspective. Yes, it is still tedious work picking a bucket of huckleberries and cleaning them afterwards, but the rewards of my labor far outweigh any of the work or discomfort involved. The beautiful mountain scenery, the sights and sounds of wildlife and the anticipation of freshly made huckleberry pancakes, cobbler, muffins and pies make the entire process worth the effort.

As I labor for the Lord, my life's experiences will not always going be pleasant. Even through the difficult times, I need to keep the right perspective knowing that my Lord will reward my faithfulness.

Prayer

Heavenly Father, I pray that my life's work will be worthy of the rewards You have promised for those who toil for You. Amen.

AUGUST 31
DAY 243

*The LORD satisfies your desires with good things so
that your youth is renewed like the eagle's.*
PSALM 103:5

Antioxidants

Death is one appointment no human will miss. To man's credit, life expectancy has risen, and the quality of our golden years has improved. If you have the money, you can spend thousands of dollars on cosmetic surgeries to keep yourself looking young. They now have hip replacements and knee replacements to keep us going. However, not all the money in the world nor all the surgeries available will keep us from dying. For myself I will stick with exercising and eating healthy, including eating huckleberries, which are full of antioxidants, which help prevent cellular deterioration.

The true fountain of youth is found in my Lord and Savior Jesus Christ. He promises to give me the strength I need to fulfill the plans He has for me. In addition, when I have completed my ministry here on earth, He promises I will pass from death unto eternal life with Him in heaven.

Prayer

Dear Heavenly Father, help me to live a healthy life so that I can serve You into my elderly years. Thank You for the hope of everlasting life with You in heaven. Amen.

SEPTEMBER 1

DAY 244

*And when he had given thanks, he broke it and said, "This is
my body, which is for you; do this in remembrance of me."*
—1 CORINTHIANS 11:24

Puffy White Clouds

Day or night, one of the first things I do when I step outside is look
up at the sky. There is very little man-made light where I live, so on a
clear night with no moon, the skies are perfect for stargazing. I enjoy
watching storm fronts come and go. My favorite sky during the day is
when puffy white cumulus clouds are floating across the backdrop of
deep blue. This always reminds me of my granddaughter and the day
she made the comment how she too liked looking at those clouds.

I think it is good to have pictures or mementos that remind me of
pleasant memories of the past. Jesus never wanted me to forget what He
did for me on the cross. Therefore, He instructed the church to take
part in the eating and drinking of bread and juice to remind me how
He sacrificed His body and blood to free me from the debt of sin.

Prayer

*Thank You, Heavenly Father, for restoring man to You through
Your Son. Help me to fill my mind with only good things so
that all my memories will be pleasing to You. Amen.*

SEPTEMBER 2

DAY 245

*Do not love the world or anything in the world. If anyone
loves the world, the love of the Father is not in him.*
1 JOHN 2:15

Mouse Traps

When we bought our home the man who owned it before us told us
the house was mouse proof. This really caught the attention of my wife,
because she will not tolerate a mouse in the house. I must say his statement

was true. Only when I put black drainage pipes onto the spouting to help drain the water away from the house did a few field mice take advantage of this point of entry. The mice were caught in mousetraps and the pipes were sealed with screening to prevent anymore from coming in.

My cabin is a completely different story. I have it critter proof for anything bigger than a red squirrel. For the mice I control their infiltration by having traps set and checking on them every other day. My bait of choice is a smashed jellybean.

The world is full of pitfalls, traps and temptations. Satan knows exactly what weaknesses every Christian faces. He will use whatever bait or circumstance he needs to cause me to stumble and lose fellowship with my Heavenly Father. He wants to render me ineffective in leading others to the saving knowledge of the Gospel.

Prayer

Heavenly Father, give me a discerning spirit so I will be able to see well in advance any traps my adversary is trying to set for me. Help me to keep my eyes on You and not on the world. Amen.

SEPTEMBER 3
DAY 246

Jesus said, "For judgment I have come into this world, so that the blind will see and those who see will become blind."
JOHN 9:39

Blinded by the Light

I have heard and read articles of people involved in an automobile accident because they could not see due to the sun. I know that sounds like an oxymoron. You would think the sun would help you see well. But anyone who has driven long enough can understand how such an accident can occur. There are certain times of year when I drive home from work that I am blinded by the sunlight. It usually occurs as I crest over the top a hill that puts me directly in line with the setting sun.

The persecutor of Christians, Saul, was blinded by the light at the time of his conversion (Acts 9:3-8). Jesus is the light of the world. Even though the Light is in the world through creation, God's Word and the church there are still many who remain spiritually blinded.

Prayer

Dear Heavenly Father, help me to let my light shine brightly for You so that others will see their need to reconcile their lives with You. Amen.

SEPTEMBER 4
DAY 247

So Jeremiah took another scroll and gave it to the scribe Baruch son of Neriah, and as Jeremiah dictated, Baruch wrote on it all of the words of the scroll that Jehoiakim king of Judah had burned in the fire.
JEREMIAH 36:32

Pocket Full of Notes

There is seldom a day that goes by in which I do not have notes in my pocket. I have gotten into the habit of writing my thoughts down on a small piece of paper and placing them in my pants pocket for safekeeping. I enjoy writing songs, so when an idea pops into my head, I write it down. Certain jobs at work allow me to think of ideas for songs, books, devotionals, or even things I want to tell Carol over the dinner table. My thoughts are fleeting; if I do not write them down, they are gone forever.

The Word of God is the number one selling book year in and year out. If I did not have the Bible as my standard for living life, I would be without direction. "Heaven and earth will pass away, but my words will never pass away" (Matt. 24:35).

Prayer

Heavenly Father, I am so grateful to have Your written Word. Thank You for preserving Your words from the beginning unto eternity. Amen.

SEPTEMBER 5

DAY 248

Believe me when I say that I am in the Father and the Father is in me; or at least believe on the evidence of the miracles themselves.
JOHN 14:11

Beliefs

God did not expect me to be sinless before I accepted Jesus as my personal Savior. I will never be perfect until I receive my glorified body after passing through the doorway of death. As I read God's Word, I will begin to establish fixed beliefs on how God wants me to live my life. Once convicted to clean up a certain area of my life, I must try my best to follow through so I will not compromise my set beliefs.

This is true for reaching other goals in my life, such as building a log cabin. Once I was convinced or believed I could do it, it was then up to me to follow through on those beliefs to accomplish the task.

Prayer

Heavenly Father, I pray that You will continue to convict me in areas of my life that need to be changed so that I can accomplish the plans You have for me. Amen.

SEPTEMBER 6
DAY 249

*Do not merely listen to the word, and so
deceive yourselves. Do what it says.*
JAMES 1:22

Reading Books about Log Cabins

I know people who read several books a week. I remember when I was a child my parents worried I was not reading enough. Reading helps me to build my vocabulary, I learn about history or it can instruct me on how to do something. It is true that reading will give me knowledge, but what good is knowledge if I do not use it? I could have read every book or article written by man on how to build a log cabin, but that would not have built me one.

The apostle James puts it this way, "Do what it says." Simply reading the Bible or listening to the preacher's sermons every Sunday will not make me more Christlike unless I apply to my life what I have read or heard.

Prayer

Dear Heavenly Father, help me to be a doer of Your Word. Let my actions be a testimony of the faith I have in You. Amen.

SEPTEMBER 7
DAY 250

*Jesus said to them, "Come and have breakfast." None
of the disciples dared ask him, "Who are you?" They
knew it was the Lord. Jesus came, took the bread and
gave it to them, and did the same with the fish.*
JOHN 21:12-13

Fish for Breakfast

Some of my earliest and fondest memories as a child revolve around the activity of fishing. When I was able to tie a hook onto a fishing line and put a worm on the end of it, I was fishing. As a teenager, my Dad introduced me to fly-fishing. To this day, fly-fishing is my favorite technique for catching fish. When my nephew comes up for turkey hunting in the spring, we go fly fishing in the afternoons. We usually release everything we catch but on occasion, I will keep two for breakfast the following morning

One of my favorite moments of Jesus with His disciples was when He appeared to them for the third time after His resurrection. As the encounter is recalled, Jesus had prepared a breakfast of fish and bread from them on the shoreline of the Sea of Tiberius. I can only imagine the camaraderie, intimacy and conversation shared during this time between Jesus and His disciples.

Prayer

> *Dear Lord, I am grateful that You are there for me at any time and cherish those Spirit-filled times when You are guiding me and giving me direction. Amen.*

SEPTEMBER 8
DAY 251

"Do you not say, 'Four months more and then the harvest'? I tell you, open your eyes and look at the fields! They are ripe for harvest."
JOHN 4:35

Harvest Time

This is the time of year when fresh fruit and vegetables are a main part of our daily diet. The apple trees are full for both the human and deer to consume. The blueberries have been picked, and by this time, we have eaten locally grown sweet corn, cantaloupes, watermelons, BLTs with fresh tomatoes and zucchini. I truly enjoy this time of year when I get the chance to enjoy the harvest of those who have labored in the fields.

Every Sunday when I leave my church, I am entering into my mission field. Whether it is at work or play, with your neighbor or your family, there are plenty of opportunities for me to share the Good News of Christ. Jesus said, "The fields are ripe for harvest."

Prayer

> *Heavenly Father, help me to be constantly aware of those I encounter throughout my daily life who need Jesus as their personal Savior. Use me to help harvest lost souls for Your kingdom. Amen.*

SEPTEMBER 9
DAY 252

"If someone's offering is a fellowship offering, and he offers an animal from the herd, whether male or female, he is to present before the LORD an animal without defect."
LEVITICUS 3:1

Fresh Is the Best

America truly is the land of plenty. All across the land our grocery stores are stocked full of an endless variety of foods that are canned, frozen, boxed, bottled or bagged. Throughout most of the year, I depend on the preserving process used by manufacturers to keep my fruits and vegetables edible. Try as they may, they will never compare to freshly picked and prepared fruits and vegetables. Now that I am an adult, my taste buds have matured from carving penny candy to a vegetable tray. I would take a plate of slightly cooked hand picked asparagus over a candy bar every time. Fresh is truly the best.

My Heavenly Father wants me to give my best to Him. In the Old Testament God wanted his people to sacrifice animals without defects and wanted the best grain for offerings. I do not give burnt offerings to God but He still wants me to give Him my best effort in being obedient. With the world vying for my attention in so many areas of my life, God often gets the leftovers of my time.

Prayer

> *Heavenly Father, I pray that everything I do will be done to my utmost for Your glory, to be used by You as a witness to those who do not know You. Amen.*

SEPTEMBER 10
DAY 253

"Can anyone hide in secret places so that I cannot see him?" declares the LORD. "Do not I fill heaven and earth?" declares the LORD.
JEREMIAH 23:24

Dad's Favorite Cast Iron Pan

I could not have a cabin without having a set of cast iron cookware. My earliest recollection of a cast iron pan takes me back to my childhood. I grew up right when Teflon and steel pans were becoming popular and cast iron cookware was fading out. Nevertheless, my father did have one cast iron pan that he fried his eggs in every morning. He had the pan seasoned just right so his over-light eggs would slide right onto his plate. Well, when we kids were tall enough to reach the stove controls, we loved making fried baloney sandwiches using Dad's favorite pan. The next time Dad made his eggs they would stick. Then we would hear Dad growling, "Who used my pan?" We could never figure out how Dad knew we used his pan especially after we cleaned it so good with soap and water.

My Heavenly Father is all knowing. He knows my heart's intentions and the reason for my every action. There is no place on earth where I can hide from God. No matter how hard I try to clean myself up and look good before men, God knows the sins of my heart.

Prayer

> *Heavenly Father, help me to live my life in a way that will be pleasing to You. Therefore, there will be no need for You to hide Your face from me (Isa. 59:2). Amen.*

❦

SEPTEMBER 11
DAY 254

For it is by grace you have been saved, through faith—and this not from yourselves, it is the gift of God—not by works, so that no one can boast.
EPHESIANS 2:8-9

Soap and Water

As children, we did not know that washing Dad's favorite pan with soap and water would cause his eggs to stick the next time he used it. You cannot clean cast iron cookware as you do most of your other pots and pans; all you need to use is hot water and a scrubby, then when dry rub the cooking surface with a little vegetable oil. If you try to clean your cast iron cookware in any other way, you will ruin the finish and your pots and pans will not work properly.

Sin is what separates man from God. Many people look clean but are not truly clean from sin. I used to think I could wash my sins away by doing good works such as going to church, praying, and good deeds. The blood of Jesus and a personal relationship with Him is the only way for me to have my sins truly washed away.

Prayer

> *Thank You, Heavenly Father, for providing a way for me to be spotless from sin in Your eyes. Thank You, Jesus, for Your ultimate sacrifice and the power of Your cleansing blood. Amen.*

SEPTEMBER 12

DAY 255

God, who knows the heart, showed that he accepted them by giving the Holy Spirit to them, just as he did to us. He made no distinction between us and them, for he purified their hearts by faith.
ACTS 15:8-9

Seasoning Cast Iron Cookware

Carol got me my first Dutch oven for my forty-ninth birthday. It came with instructions on how to season it and some simple recipes. To season it, I pre-set our oven to 450 degrees. Using a paper towel, I had to spread shortening over the entire surface of the cast iron oven. I then put it in the oven for one hour. I took the cookware out of the oven, and using a paper towel, I coated the inside of the Dutch oven with shortening. After cooling down, my cast iron cookware would be prepared for its first of many mouth-watering meals.

I need to cover my entire life in faith so I can rest assured my heart will be purified in the eyes of my Heavenly Father. Once my heart is right with God, I will be able to spread the Good News with those who cross my path.

Prayer

Dear Heavenly Father, I pray that I will be faithful in my walk with You so that my heart may remain pure in Your sight. Amen.

SEPTEMBER 13
DAY 256

*Don't let anyone look down on you because you
are young, but set an example for the believers in
speech, in life, in love, in faith and in purity.*
1 TIMOTHY 4:12

Dutch Oven Cooking

I will never forget the day I was introduced to Dutch oven cooking. It was during the Christmas holidays of 2004. I received a phone call from our friend's son-in-law, and he asked if I would be interested in seeing a demonstration on how to cook up a couple of desserts using a Dutch oven. The charcoal briquettes were already burning and the baking ingredients were on the table when Carol and I arrived. I helped him mix up a chocolate cake, cherry cobbler and pineapple upside down cake. Then we started baking. When he turned over the Dutch oven and a perfectly baked pineapple upside down cake lay on the lid of the oven I was hooked. Our friend's son-in-law's example leads me to enjoy the wonderful world of cooking outside with cast iron cookware.

As a Christian, I too need to lead by example. They world is watching me. I know because they are the first to tell me when I do something wrong. Leading by example will give me opportunities to share my faith.

Prayer

Heavenly Father, help me to be aware of every opportunity You give me to share the gospel and give me the words to explain the Good News clearly. Amen.

SEPTEMBER 14
DAY 257

*You became imitators of us and of the Lord; in spite of severe suffering,
you welcomed the message with the joy given by the Holy Spirit.*
1 THESSALONIANS 1:6

Just Like a Conventional Oven

Dutch ovens are very versatile. I can make a greater variety of food in my Dutch oven than any other cooking utensil found in the household. I can use it as a deep fryer, a stewing pan, pressure cooker, frying pan, and its unique aspect, as an oven, hence the name Dutch oven. When I am camping, having a Dutch oven as part of my outfit is just like packing a conventional oven and bringing it along. I can bake cakes or prepare casseroles; there is no limit on what can be on the camp menu.

My goal as a Christian is to become more like Jesus with each passing day. When people meet me they need to see and feel the same love Jesus had for the world, a love so great that He sacrificed His life for me.

Prayer

Dear Father in heaven, I pray that I will be just like Your Son, Jesus. Help me to do what Jesus would do in the circumstances I face each day. Amen.

SEPTEMBER 15

DAY 258

Anyone who lives on milk, being still an infant, is not acquainted with the teaching about righteousness. But solid food is for the mature, who by constant use have trained themselves to distinguish good from evil.
HEBREWS 5:13-14

All Charcoal Is Not the Same

When baking with a Dutch oven, I place hot charcoal briquettes under the oven and on top of the lid. Not all charcoal is created equal. Different brands of charcoal burn hotter and longer than their competition. Experience has taught me how many briquettes of a certain brand I need to get the desired results.

Not all believers in Christ are created equal. We are all at different levels of growth in our spiritual walks. Experience in following God's commands and fellowshiping with other believers will help me to burn hotter for Him.

Prayer

Heavenly Father, help me to be discerning in determining the conviction of other believers. Help me to be patient and understanding with believers who are taking their first baby steps in their spiritual journey. Amen.

SEPTEMBER 16

DAY 259

How sweet are your words to my taste,
sweeter than honey to my mouth!
PSALM 119:103

Dutch Ovens Feed the Pioneers

There is nothing fancy about cast iron cookware. From the little I know of its history, the Dutch are credited with creating some of the best pieces of cast iron cookware. Cast iron cookware is black and heavy to lift. To simply look at a piece, next to a new shiny modern day pot or pan you would probably buy the new version. However, truth be told, if seasoned properly and maintained they will serve you well in all your cooking endeavors. They provided many a hot meal for cold, tired and hungry pioneers traveling and settling across a great nation of ours.

Bibles were at one time nothing fancy to look at, not like our study Bibles of today. They usually had a black cover with God's Word in between. Those Bibles fed many a believer and started many a revival. Remember you can't judge a book by its cover.

Prayer

Thank You, Heavenly Father, for the black-covered book I call the Bible, and thank You for the life-changing words in between that have brought many a person, including myself, to the saving knowledge of Jesus. Amen

SEPTEMBER 17
DAY 260

Listen to my instruction and be wise; do not ignore it.
PROVERBS 8:33

Following the Formula

When using charcoal briquettes there is a formula to determine how many briquettes to use to maintain a temperature of 350 degrees for one hour. Multiply the diameter of your oven by two; if you were using a twelve-inch oven your answer would be twenty-four. This is how many charcoal briquettes you would need to use. Then you place two-thirds on the lid and one-third underneath your oven, which in this case would be sixteen on top and eight on the bottom. Knowing what temperature I am baking at helps my recipes to turn out right.

The Bible is God's instructions for man to follow. It is God's desire for me to follow His commands correctly. If I do this, the plans God has for my life will turn out the way He desires.

Prayer

> *Thank You, Heavenly Father, for Your written principles on how to live a victorious life. Help me to carefully follow Your instructions for a spirit-filled life so that I will fulfill the plans You have for me. Amen.*

SEPTEMBER 18
DAY 261

Now Israel loved Joseph more than any of his other sons, because he had been born to him in his old age; and he made a richly ornamented robe for him.
GENESIS 37:3

The Many Colors of Fall

I went to work this morning and I noticed the leaves from the trees already beginning to cover the roadway. I have an hour-long commute to work through some of the best mountain scenery offered in Pennsylvania. I have a front row view of the comings and goings of our four seasons. Fall, without a doubt, is my favorite to watch arrive. No matter how closely I watch the leaves turning to their fall colors, it seems like they all change over night. I will be driving home from work and instead of looking at lush green mountainsides I will be treated to a sunlit mountainside of multi-colored foliage

One of my favorite characters in the Bible is known for having a multi-colored coat. Of course, I am speaking of Joseph. He is an example for me to do my best for God no matter what my circumstances. Whether as a servant, a prisoner or second only to pharaoh, Joseph trusted God and God was with him.

Prayer

> *Dear Heavenly Father, no matter how minor or prestigious a job may be, I pray I will do it for Your glory and not for my desired appraisal of others. Amen.*

SEPTEMBER 19
DAY 262

And not to steal from them, but to show that they can be fully trusted, so that in every way they will make the teaching about God our Savior attractive.
TITUS 2:10

Fall Colors Attract Many People to the Mountains

The window of opportunity to see the fall colors at their peak is usually about two weeks. It is during these two weeks that many people take long Sunday drives or come up for a weekend and stay at their cabin. The mountains, full of color, have a way of drawing people out of their homes and into the hills. It is a joyful and refreshing time for family and friends to enjoy the beauty of God's creation.

The way I live my life should be attractive to the people around me. Everything I do and every word out of my mouth should be done and said in a way to draw others to the love of Christ. Through my example, others should want to experience the same joy I have in my life.

Prayer

> *Heavenly Father, when the door of opportunity opens, help me explain the Good News with those who are lost. Amen.*

SEPTEMBER 20
DAY 263

*Splendor and majesty are before him; strength
and glory are in his sanctuary.*
PSALM 96:6

Fall Splendor

Webster defines splendor as the quality of being magnificent, glorious or sumptuous, also as an instance or display of imposing pomp, grandeur, brilliance or radiance. Webster's definition hits the nail on the head when describing the peak of coloration during the fall foliage in the mountains. It is magnificent. It truly is an imposing display. The words pop, grandeur, brilliance and radiance are all words that can be used to describe the beauty of fall foliage.

I am supposed to worship God in the splendor of His holiness. Man has never seen the face of God. The radiance of God caused Moses' face to be so radiant that he needed to put a veil over his face. It is hard for man to imagine God in His entire splendor with his finite mind.

Prayer

Dear Heavenly Father, I am grateful that You are perfect and holy. Let me live my life hating sin so I may better see You throughout my days here on earth. Amen.

SEPTEMBER 21
DAY 264

Now, brothers, I want to remind you of the gospel I preached to you, which you received and on which you have taken your stand. By this gospel you are saved.
1 CORINTHIANS 15:1–2

Keep It Simple

I am fifty years old and falling quickly behind the technological curve. Not because I am mentally incapable of keeping up, but rather because I choose not to get caught up in every new advancement that comes out. Technology is supposed to make things easier to do so I have more time to do things I want. The more I get caught up in every new gadget that hits the market the less time I have to do the activities I enjoy. Carol and I boxed up the computer so we could spend more time with one another and do things like putting a jigsaw puzzle together. I enjoy taking long walks in the mountains and sitting around a campfire. We decided we are going to enjoy the simpler things in life.

The plan of salvation God has put in place to be reconciled to Him is truly simple. "Believe in the Lord Jesus, and you will be saved" (Acts 16:31). After I came to know Jesus as my personal Savior, it made me wonder how I could have been so blind for so long to such a simple message.

Prayer

> *Thank You, Heavenly Father, for opening my eyes so I was able to see my way to You. Help me to explain the gospel to others who do not know You in such a way that they too will see the truth clearly. Amen.*

SEPTEMBER 22
Day 265

If your brother sins against you, go and show him
his fault, just between the two of you. If he listens
to you, you have won your brother over.
MATTHEW 18:15

Gathering Fallen Leaves

The colorful fall foliage only lasts for a short time. Then the varied shades of red, yellow, and orange all begin to turn brown. Once the leaves turn brown, you know it will not be long before the leaves start falling to the ground. With the combination of rain, wind, and the first frost of the year, the trees seem to defoliate over night. Once on the ground the annual chore of gathering up the leaves begins. This is not a job I look forward to doing, but it is necessary to keep ditches and gutters open for water to pass through.

There will be times when brothers and sisters in Christ whom I know will fall out of fellowship from God for one reason or another. Even though it is not always pleasant to do, it is God's desire for me to gather those fallen from His graces and bring them back to the flock through prayer, love, and compassion. It is my hope they will see the errors of their ways and will be revealed and repent of their sins.

Prayer

> *Dear Heavenly Father, help me to have the compassion shown by Jesus when He dealt with sinners. Remind me where I once was and use me to bring back believers who have fallen out of fellowship with You. Amen.*

SEPTEMBER 23
DAY 266

Let us draw near to God with a sincere heart in full assurance of faith, having our hearts sprinkled to cleanse us from a guilty conscience and having our bodies washed with pure water.
HEBREWS 10:22

Cold Days Draw People Closer to the Fire

The cabin is near completion. There are a few details that need done but the end is in sight and the goal for completing the cabin by the end of October will be attained.

Now is the time of year I like building a fire in the fire ring outside of the cabin. I enjoy feeling the warmth of the fire as the temperatures begin to fall at sunset. Fire has a way of drawing people together, especially on a cold day. The colder it gets the closer everyone gets to the fire to stay warm.

God wants me to draw near to Him. It is His desire to keep me close to His heart. If God seems distant, it is not because God has moved, rather I have moved away from God.

Prayer

Heavenly Father, it is my prayer to continually come to know You better so that my life will attract others to You. Amen.

SEPTEMBER 24
DAY 267

Do not put out the Spirit's fire.
1 THESSALONIANS 5:19

Wood is a Good Source for Heat

They say, "When you heat with wood you get warmed up twice." Once from cutting, splitting, and stacking, then again when you burn it. Usually sometime before the end of September I will fire up the wood-burning stove to take the chill or dampness out of the air. It does not take long for the inside temperature of the house to go from the low sixties to the mid-eighties. Wood is a good source of heat when burned and is plentiful where I live.

The world has a way of cooling my spiritual embers. I need to keep my body, the temple of the Holy Spirit, free from worldly desires that can extinguish the fire of the Holy Spirit. I want the Holy Spirit to burn hot so my desire to serve my Heavenly Father will never cool.

Prayer

Dear Heavenly Father, help me not to be distracted by all the worldly pleasures, but rather walk in the Spirit so I continue to have a burning desire to serve You. Amen.

SEPTEMBER 25
DAY 268

*And the words of the Lord are flawless, like silver
refined in a furnace of clay, purified seven times.*
PSALM 12:6

Fire Purifies

If you were with me while I was cooking out at the cabin, you might hear me say, "A little dirt will never hurt." I never know when a foreign object such as an ash or piece of bark will fall into my fixin's. I have a theory that if I ingest a few germs it will help keep my immune system functioning properly. As long as the food I am preparing is good and hot, the chances for any bacteria or germ to survive are nil. I have never had any cases of food poisoning at camp. Fire has a way of purifying; for instance, if you boil water, it is then okay to consume, and the Bible speaks of purifying silver by burning out the impurities over a fire.

God desires for me to have a pure heart. I should continually pray to God to reveal any sin I need to confess. My heart is like a window, the cleaner it is from sin the better I will be able to see God (Matt. 5:8).

Prayer

*Dear Heavenly Father, I pray that You reveal to me any sin I
need to reconcile with You. Give me a pure heart so that I may
see You plainly. Amen.*

SEPTEMBER 26
DAY 269

*For a thousand years in your sight are like a day that
has just gone by, or like a watch in the night.*
PSALM 90:4

Biological Clocks

Animals do not revolve their lives around a clock like us humans do. Yet without instruments of time, built-in biological clocks help our furry and feathery friends dictate what they need to do before the arrival of winter. Some birds change color and stay for the winter, while other birds begin their migration south. The bears are busy getting their last meals before a long winter rest, and squirrels scurry to build up a food supply that will last until the arrival of spring. For the white-tailed deer, it is time to breed and grow their winter coats. All this is done without the use of a clock.

God's timing is not my timing. It makes me wonder if it was ever God's desire for man to use calendars and timepieces to measure time. It seems to me man has become a slave to time itself. I become impatient with God when my prayers are not answered in a timely manner. I try to be careful not to put God into an hourglass; the Bible tells me a thousand years is like one day to God.

Prayer

Heavenly Father, help me not to become a slave to time but rather use the time You have given me to serve You in everything I do, think, and say. In Jesus' name, I pray. Amen.

SEPTEMBER 27
DAY 270

"But in those days, following that distress, 'the sun will be darkened, and the moon will not give its light; the stars will fall from the sky, and the heavenly bodies will be shaken.' At that time men will see the Son of Man coming in clouds with great power and glory."
MARK 13:24–26

Apple Cider and Ginger Snaps

The signs of the passing of summer and the coming of fall are many: the changing of the leaves, buck rubs on saplings, college football, dropping temperatures, and the grass finally stops growing. The truest sign of fall for me is a tradition that I keep each fall. That is the drinking of apple cider while eating a ginger snap. The combination has to be consumed together for the ultimate enjoyment on the taste buds. When this is done I always say, "Yes, fall is now here."

Jesus said there would be signs to look for before He returns. He also said false prophets claiming to be the Christ would deceive many. The Bible tells me trumpets will sound, lightning will flash, and the Son of Man will come on a cloud. I look with anticipation for the return of Jesus.

Prayer

Thank You, Jesus, for leaving Your heavenly home to save mankind on Your first coming. I look forward to when You will take your bride, the church, back home with You to heaven. Amen.

SEPTEMBER 28
DAY 271

For the wages of sin is death, but the gift of God is eternal life in Christ Jesus our Lord.
ROMANS 6:23

Gift from a Friend

My original plan for heating the cabin was to build a fireplace. The more I read on the constructing of fireplaces the less feasible that became. The main deterrents for not building a fireplace were the time involved and not having a good draft after building the firebox and flue. My decision not to build a fireplace was confirmed when my friend offered me a free wood-burning stove.

Mankind has received gifts from God. Eternal life through Jesus Christ and the Holy Spirit, Jesus said He would send after His ascension into heaven. God has offered these gifts to the world, but it is man's responsibility to take the gifts.

Prayer

> *Thank You, Heavenly Father, for Your gifts of eternal life and the Holy Spirit. Help me to be forever grateful for what it cost You to provide those gifts for me. Amen.*

SEPTEMBER 29
DAY 272

Come, O house of Jacob, let us walk in the light of the Lord.
ISAIAH 2:5

Walking in the Woods

With all the chores of summer and the building of the log cabin slowly coming to an end, I can finally get back to one of my favorite activities: taking long walks in the woods. I pack lightly, taking only a bottle of water, an apple, a topographical map of the area I am walking, and my compass. I have 25,000 square acres of state game land to explore behind my house. The purposes of these walks are many. I enjoy the solitude, it is good exercise, and it allows me to scout for new areas to hunt, but mainly I enjoy the time with God while observing His creation.

It is my Heavenly Father's desire for me to walk with Him in all of my daily activities. The closer I walk with my Lord, the better I will know Him and the clearer I will hear Him when He talks to me.

Prayer

> *Heavenly Father, I pray that each step I take will bring me closer to You. Help me not to stray from Your righteous path. Amen.*

SEPTEMBER 30
DAY 273

The man who has accepted it has certified that God is truthful.
JOHN 3:33

Dream Come True

I will never forget the first night I built a fire in the wood-burning stove. We had our friends over for a cast iron skillet evening meal while sitting around a fire in the fire ring. It was getting dark when we decided it would be a good time to check the draft in the wood-burning stove. It did not take long to get flames flickering in the stove. The wood burner opens in the front with two doors inlaid with glass. While we sat outside and looked in the open cabin door, it was like a dream come true seeing the light of the flames dancing off the walls of the cabin.

There is nothing more true than God and His Word. God tells me that He is truth. There are people who search for truth all their lives. It gives me great peace knowing the integrity of God in uncompromising and all my dreams will come true if I live according to His plan for me.

Prayer

> *Dear Heavenly Father, I am so grateful for Your word and Your sinless character. It gives me great comfort knowing that You are a God of truth, and I want all the plans You have for me to come true. Amen.*

OCTOBER 1
Day 274

When I was a child, I talked like a child, I thought
like a child, I reasoned like a child. When I became
a man, I put childish ways behind me.
1 CORINTHIANS 13:11

Pile of Leaves

My wife accuses me of having Peter Pan syndrome. I must admit I do have childish flashbacks, like when I try to do a cartwheel or some other stunt I used to do as a kid just to see if I can still do it, or when I throw a piece of paper away in the trash like I'm shooting a basketball. Raking the leaves into a big pile each year always stirs in me the temptation of running and jumping into the middle of the big pile just as I did as a child.

It is okay to remain young at heart; however, this does not mean I should continue to act like a child. It is God's desire for me to put my childish ways behind me. I need to be mature in Christ so I can be a Godly example to my children and the children and youth I teach in Sunday school.

Prayer

Heavenly Father, I pray that I never lose a childlike enthusiasm for life. Help me to touch the lives of young people in such a way that they would desire to dedicate their lives to You. Amen.

OCTOBER 2
Day 275

Your word is a lamp to my feet and a light for my path.
PSALM 119:105

Flashlight

For me the best time to sit around a campfire is at night, because I can see better all the different colors in the flames and the glowing of the hot coals. It also is a little cooler at night so the warmth of the fire feels better. When sitting around the fire with friends, it is usually ten o'clock before we call it a night, at which time I take a large bucket of water and put out the fire. Now, as you can imagine, it is completely dark. In order to find our way back to the house, I use a flashlight to light up the path for everyone to stay on.

I live in a dark world. In order for me to stay on the narrow way that leads to joyful life, I need to study the Word of God. God's Word will light up my path and keep me on track.

Prayer

> *Dear Heavenly Father, thank You for Your infallible Word and for opening my eyes to Your truths to illuminate my way through a dark world. Amen.*

OCTOBER 3
DAY 276

"Therefore keep watch, because you do not know on what day your Lord will come."
MATTHEW 24:42

Standing Watch

Smokey the Bear says, "Only you can prevent forest fires." The last thing I want to do is start a forest fire. Besides the hefty fine, I would hate to see the loss of habitat and my beautiful stand of pines go up in flames. I am very careful whenever I burn trash or have a fire at the cabin in the fire ring. I use a screen over the burn barrel to prevent hot ashes from coming out, and at the fire ring I always stand watch with a bucket of water handy to extinguish any sparks outside the metal ring.

One of the great truths of Christianity is the belief that Jesus is going to return. Looking for the return of Jesus helps me live a Godly life. I do not want to be caught in some worldly activity at the second coming of Jesus. I need to be vigilant in my watch for the glorious return of Jesus to earth.

Prayer

> *Heavenly Father, help me to keep my eyes on Jesus. I pray my focus is on Him and I am bringing Him glory in every activity I partake up to His triumphant return. Amen.*

OCTOBER 4

DAY 277

The mind of sinful man is death, but the mind controlled by the Spirit is life and peace; the sinful mind is hostile to God.
ROMANS 8:6–7

Wildfire

The fire ring I have at the cabin is the rim from the tire of an eighteen-wheel tractor-trailer. I have the rim surrounded with mountain stone. I keep a rake in the cabin to keep the area free of any pine needles or limbs that have fallen around the fire ring from my last fire. In addition, when I have a fire, I always have a bucket of water nearby to extinguish any stray sparks. If it has been dry for several weeks, I will not even start a fire down at the cabin. Fire is a good thing when it is under control but a fire out of control is devastating to everything it consumes.

The sinful nature of man is like a wildfire that leads to death. The Christian, however, is controlled by the Spirit of God who lives in us. If I let the Holy Spirit control me, He will lead me to a life of peace and eternal life.

Prayer

> *Heavenly Father, I pray my actions are always under control, and self would not interfere with the workings of the Holy Spirit in my life. Amen.*

OCTOBER 5
Day 278

By all this we are encouraged. In addition to our own encouragement, we were especially delighted to see how happy Titus was, because his spirit has been refreshed by all of you.
2 Corinthians 7:13

Falls Cool Breeze

If you were to give Carol and me a choice between winter and summer, we would both pick winter. I know that probably goes against the majority but we both enjoy the colder temperatures and longer evenings. That is why all the windows are open to let those first cool breezes of fall to pass through the house. The laundry blown dry on the wash line smells fresher and I have a little more get up in my get go. To us the colder temperatures are much more refreshing than the oppressive climate of summer.

It is wise for me to restore my spirit. It does not take long for the daily activities of my life to tire me out. Therefore, whether it is through a friend, music, quiet time with God, or even a leisurely walk by myself, I need to take time each day to revive my spirit.

Prayer

Help me, Heavenly Father, to energize my spirit daily. Also, help me to be an instrument used by You to rejuvenate the spirit of other believers. Amen.

OCTOBER 6
DAY 279

If you belonged to the world, it would love you as its own.
As it is, you do not belong to the world, but I have chosen
you out of the world. That is why the world hates you.
JOHN 15:19

Warm but Cold

When it is hot outside, I can only take off so many clothes to stay cooler. Then, when I do this, I compound the problem by getting sunburn on skin that has not been exposed since the previous summer. This is another reason I like the cooler temperatures. I call fall and winter "sweater weather." I dress in layers at this time of year. This way I can add or take off a layer of clothing to stay comfortable. I can dress so that no matter how cold it is outside my body will still be warm.

When I accepted Jesus as my personal Savior, I immediately became part of the Kingdom of God. I am no longer part of the world. I am saved, but still in the world. Living in the world is just part of my eternal life until I pass through the doorway of death into my home in heaven.

Prayer

Thank You, dear Heavenly Father, for the comfort of knowing that even though I am in the world my eternal life has already begun. I look forward to inhabiting the place prepared for me with You in heaven. Amen.

OCTOBER 7
DAY 280

On this day atonement will be made for you, to cleanse you.
Then, before the LORD, you will be clean from all your sins.
LEVITICUS 16:30

Clean Up

The day has finally come to start cleaning up around the cabin. Tools I used all summer long can now be put back where they belong. Piles of peeled bark and chips of wood need raked up and wheelbarreled away. Dead limbs and pine needles have to be gathered and taken away. The inside of the cabin floor needs a good sweeping from all the wood dust made by the bore worms. Keeping a clean cabin and campsite is a job that needs done regularly.

As I live out my Christina life in a dirty world, it is necessary for me to clean out any worldly clutter I may have accumulated along the way. Nothing that is not pleasing to God should be a part of my daily life. I need to examine my heart to make sure there is not any sin that has to be forgiven. I need to keep my vessel clean to be used by God.

Prayer

> *Heavenly Father, it is my only desire to be used by You for Your glory. I pray my temple would be kept clean so that You can dwell within me. Amen.*

OCTOBER 8
DAY 281

In a desert land he found him, in a barren and howling waste.
DEUTERONOMY 32:10

Camp Name

Now that the cabin was near completion, it was time to give the camp a name. For example, I named my parents' home "Kamp Komfort" while hunting out of it. Other examples of cabin names in our area are "Whispering Pines," "Buckhorn," "West End," and "Fear Not," just to name a few. I had no idea for a camp name, then one evening while sitting around the fire, my friend mentioned a verse he read from his KJV Bible, Deuteronomy 32:10, that mentioned the howling wilderness. As our conversation continued, I realized that would be a great name for my cabin.

There are many names associated with God in the Old Testament. My favorite, though, is found in the New Testament when Jesus tells His disciples to address God as Father. It is comforting to know I have a Heavenly Father with whom to converse.

Prayer

Heavenly Father, I dedicate the cabin to You, to be used by You as a place where You can pull on the heart strings of myself and others so we will be in better tune with You. Amen.

OCTOBER 9
DAY 282

Proclaim the power of God, whose majesty is over Israel, whose power is in the skies.
PSALM 68:34

Howling

"Howling Wilderness"—just by saying the name of the cabin it takes me to a place that is cold and remote. I like the word "howling." Anyone who knows me has heard me imitate the howling of the wind. There is something in that sound that reminds me I am not the one in control. While I am out hunting on a windy winter day, I like to face directly into the biting wind. It makes me feel alive and it helps me to appreciate how God created the animals to survive in those conditions.

The howling of the wind reminds me that I serve an all-powerful God. Man cannot control the direction, time, or strength of the wind on any give day.

Prayer

>*Dear Heavenly Father, I am grateful that You are all-powerful. Let me rely on Your strength and not on my own as I serve You in my daily life. Amen.*

OCTOBER 10
DAY 283

Your ways, O God, are holy. What god is so great as our God?
PSALM 77:13

Wilderness

By definition wilderness is a wild, comparatively uninhabited, and uncultivated region, as of forest or desert; a tract of wasteland. Wilderness is any area of land untouched by man. Even though I live in the mountains of central Pennsylvania, I would not consider this area wilderness. The trees have been harvested several times since the early 1900s. There are few virgin trees to be found. I would love to walk through an area of ground untouched by man since the creation of God.

My God is a holy God. Thankfully, man is not able to destroy the holiness of God. God will not allow any sin to blemish His purity. That is why I need Jesus in order for me to have a relationship with God. God looks at me through Jesus. The blood of Jesus washed all my sins away.

Prayer

>*Heavenly Father, You are a holy God. I pray that I give You all the reverence You deserve. Thank You for allowing me to commune with You through your Son Jesus Christ. Amen.*

OCTOBER 11

DAY 284

The workers who were hired about the eleventh hour came and each received a denarius.

MATTHEW 20:9

Late Season Trout Stocking

In October, I get my fly line wet for the last time. In the early part of October, the Fish Commission has a late stocking for trout. Weather permitting, Dad and I will meet at one of the stocked locations the following day. It gives me a good excuse to take a half day off work and enjoy some time on the trout stream with my Dad. For me, there is nothing better than a seventy degree day in October, fly-fishing a mountain stream full of trout and while enjoying fall foliage with my Dad. It is never too late to catch that final trout of the year.

It is true, a high percentage of people come to know Jesus as their personal Savior before the age of eighteen and the percentages continue to go down every year there after. It is not God's desire that anyone should perish (2 Pet. 3:9). Our God is a patient God and a God of love. It is never too late for someone to accept Jesus as his or her Savior.

Prayer

Dear Heavenly Father, as I get older I pray that You give me the wisdom and the words to touch those who are in their later years, who have not yet accepted Your plan of salvation. Amen.

OCTOBER 12
DAY 285

But seek first his kingdom and his righteousness, and all these things will be given to you as well.
MATTHEW 6:33

Hunting Season Begins

I grew up in a hunting family. From October through January at least one meal per week offered wild game as the main dish. For a boy like me, small game season was a rite of passage that began when you turned twelve years old. It was tradition for my uncles and nephews to come to my parent's home for opening day. At eight o'clock, the firehouse would sound the alarm signaling the official opening of small game season. I never thought the day would come that I too would be heading into the fields with my dad, older brother, and relatives in pursuit of pheasant and rabbits.

Man spends a lifetime pursuing happiness. Without God, man's attempt to find true happiness is futile or temporary at the best. I want my joy to be complete as promised by Jesus. God tells me to pursue first the kingdom of God and everything else will fall into place.

Prayer

Dear Lord, it is my goal to be obedient to You so that I may experience Your full measure of joy while here on earth. Amen.

OCTOBER 13

DAY 286

*There is a time for everything, and a season
for every activity under heaven.*
ECCLESIASTES 3:1

Winter, Spring, Summer, Fall

I experienced all four seasons during the construction of my log cabin—the snow and cold of winter, the blooms and rain of spring, the heat and humidity of summer, and finally the wind and frost of fall. I enjoy the uniqueness of each season. Where we live in north central Pennsylvania each season lasts three months. Therefore, it does not seem very long before one season is transforming into the next. Each season has certain qualities that are distinctive to it, that provide an individual with different activities to perform each season.

God tells me in Ecclesiastes that there is a time for everything as I go through the seasons of my life. Going from child to teenager to adult and finally into my elder years, each period provides me ways to carry out God's will and enjoy life experiences that are unique to each age group.

Prayer

Dear Heavenly Father, I pray that You give me the opportunity to live a long life so I can experience old age and be a blessing to You through each stage of my life. Amen.

OCTOBER 14
DAY 287

Then Peter came to Jesus and asked, "Lord, how many times shall I forgive my brother when he sins against me? Up to seven times?" Jesus answered, "I tell you, not seven times, but seventy-seven times."
MATTHEW 18:21–22

Twelve Times

It is that time of year when I start burning wood to stay warm. They say, "burning wood warms you up twice." Once when you split it and once when you burn it in your wood-burning stove. Well I am here to say, that saying falls a little short. By my calculations, I was warmed up six times that amount. From the time I cut the wood up from its original destination until the time I place the wood into the wood-burning stove, I have handled it twelve times.

Peter asked Jesus how many times he should forgive someone. Is there any limit on the times I should forgive someone? Is there a limit on the times Jesus will forgive sin and me when I stumble? Let me not only forgive those who transgress against me but let me forget their transgression just as my Lord and Savior would do.

Prayer

Dear Heavenly Father, let me never forget where I was before I met You. Let that be a constant reminder for me to love and forgive others as You love and forgive me. Amen.

OCTOBER 15

DAY 288

And we urge you, brothers, warn those who are idle, encourage the timid, help the weak, be patient with everyone.
1 THESSALONIANS 5:14

Don't Burn Green Wood

Wood, when burned, is a good source of heat. When I am cold, the warmth from a wood-burning stove warms me to my bones. Actually burning wood is such a good source of heat, it is not uncommon for people to have windows open in the middle of winter to bring the inside temperature down. For the best results in burning wood, I use wood that is well seasoned yet not rotten. Seasoned means all the moisture is out of the wood. Green wood is wood that was just cut from a standing tree and is full of moisture. This wood should be stacked and let sit for a year before burning in the stove.

My timing is not always God's timing. There will be times in life I need to wait patiently for God to mold me before He can fulfill the plans He has for the next stage of my life.

Prayer

Dear Lord, help me to be uncomplaining as I wait for Your timing. Help me to be patient with others. Help me to be unwearied in an impatient world. Amen.

OCTOBER 16
Day 289

*Serve wholeheartedly, as if you were serving the Lord, not
men, because you know that the Lord will reward everyone
for whatever good he does, whether he is slave or free.*
Ephesians 6:7–8

I Need Help

I needed some help with the roof and an extra hand in getting the
wood-burning stove into the cabin. It took me and my friend all the
strength we had just to lift the wood-burning stove up and onto his
truck bed. We drove from my friend's house over to mine and parked
where the trail to the cabin comes out to the driveway. The path to the
cabin from the driveway is about twenty yards. We managed to lift the
stove onto a wheelbarrow, and my friend held the stove in place while I
pulled the wheelbarrow backward to the cabin. With one final lift, we
got the stove inside the cabin and then slid it until it was finally where
I wanted it to be. There is no way I could have gotten that stove where
it needed to be with what I had without my friend's help.

A big part of being a Christian is being a servant. Each day I should
ask God to make me sensitive to meeting the needs of others, so He can
use me to be a blessing in someone's life.

Prayer

*Heavenly Father, help me to serve others with unconditional
love. Whether it is by a kind word or deed, help me to meet
the needs of those I encounter each day. Amen.*

OCTOBER 17
DAY 290

*I will remain in the world no longer, but they are still
in the world, and I am coming to you. Holy Father,
protect them by the power of your name - the name you
gave me - so that they may be one as we are one.*
JOHN 17:11

Firebricks

I needed to line the wood-burning stove with firebricks. There were
firebricks already in it but some were broken and others deteriorated
to the point of being too thin. I was able to salvage three bricks out
of the twenty I needed. I went to the brickyard and bought seventeen
firebricks to line the wood stove. It was like a jigsaw puzzle getting all
twenty bricks to fit in place. There were eight on the bottom and four
each on the two sides and back. The firebricks protect the outer walls of
the stove from the high temperatures.

The closer we walk with God the better He is able to protect me
from Satan's lies. God does not move from me but I have to be careful
I do not move from Him when my adversary turns up the heat of
temptations.

Prayer

*Dear Heavenly Father, I pray that I will line my heart with
the protection of Your Word. Thank You for your desire to
protect me from the temporary pleasures the world has to offer.
Amen.*

OCTOBER 18
Day 291

*After he said this, he was taken up before their very
eyes, and a cloud hid him from their sight.*
ACTS 1:9

Heat Rises

Hot air is lighter than cold air, so naturally hot air will rise above the cooler air. It is very difficult to force hot air down. This is why furnaces and stoves for heating are located in the basement. The heat simply rises or is forced upstairs through vents. Also, this is the reason people who have cathedral ceilings in their homes have a harder time keeping the temperature comfortable at room level. The fact that hot air rises makes it very comfortable in the loft of the cabin on cold winter nights.

The scripture for today tells how Jesus rose into heaven in front of His disciples. This was a very important event. Earlier in Jesus' ministry, he explained to the disciples that the Holy Spirit would not be sent until He had risen to be reunited with His Father.

Prayer

Dear Heavenly Father, thank You for the gift of the Holy Spirit. I pray that my body, the temple of the Holy Spirit, will be warmed by His presence in my life. Amen.

OCTOBER 19
Day 292

*In a flash, in the twinkling of an eye, at the last
trumpet. For the trumpet will sound, the dead will be
raised imperishable, and we will be changed.*
1 CORINTHIANS 15:52

Smoke Curls Skyward

Have you ever noticed that when you are the only one standing around a fire, the smoke comes in your direction? No matter which side of the fire you go on, the smoke eventually comes your way. The reason for this, so I am told, is that your body is acting like a chimney and causes a draft for the smoke to come towards you and raise skyward.

The first thing I did when I connected the wood-burning stove to the chimney was to burn a piece of newspaper to make sure I had a good draft. I knew the draft was good when I stepped outside and saw the smoke rising above the treetops.

As I looked forward with anticipation that the wood stove would have a good draft, I too look forward to the day that my soul will be reunited with my glorified body. God's Word tells me that my body will be raised to heaven. I have victory over death through my Lord and Savior Jesus Christ.

Prayer

Thank You, Heavenly Father, for Your promise of eternal life with a risen body free from aches and pain as You intended before man's fall. Amen.

OCTOBER 20
DAY 293

The one who received the seed that fell among the thorns is the man who hears the word, but the worries of this life and the deceitfulness of wealth choke it, making it unfruitful.
MATTHEW 13:22

Don't Clog the Chimney

Another reason I let wood dry is that it burns cleaner. Green wood not only burns poorly but will also line a chimney with residue quicker than dry wood. I rarely burn a piece of evergreen wood in my wood stove. Burning fir, spruce, hemlock or pine will line a chimney with creosote. Periodically I open the damper in my stove wide open so I have a hot fire. This helps keep the sides of the chimney clean.

As a Christian, I need to be careful that my witness is not choked out by sin. If I keep my spiritual embers burning hot, it will be less likely for this to happen. However, if I close out or quench the prompting of the Holy Spirit, chances are sin will quickly choke out the light of my testimony.

Prayer

Heavenly Father, I pray that my spiritual fire will continue to burn hot for You so that sin will not hamper the plans You have for me. Amen.

OCTOBER 21
DAY 294

"Whoever believes in me, as the Scripture has said, streams of living water will flow from within him." By this he meant the Spirit, whom those who believed in him were later to receive.
JOHN 7:38–39

Keep the Water Flowing

Another chore that pulled me away from my weekend cabin building was the annual cleaning up of the leaves. Those beautiful red, orange, and yellow leaves soon turn brown and with the help of the winds and rain, they quickly find themselves on the ground. Therefore, each year I get my eight-by-ten-foot tarp out and rake the leaves onto it. Then I drag the tarp in the woods and dispose of them where they can harmlessly deteriorate into soil. I do this to keep the ditches and gutter clean from leaves so rainwater and the melting snow in the spring will flow freely away from the house.

Jesus tells me in the scripture for today, that if I believe in Him streams of living water will flow from me. My life will be clean of sin and the Holy Spirit will be free to run my life in the direction God wants me to go.

Prayer

> *Dear Heavenly Father, I pray that I will be a fountain of living water, so that those living in the world without Jesus will be refreshed by the Holy Spirit living in me. Amen.*

OCTOBER 22
DAY 295

> *When Jesus spoke again to the people, he said, "I am the light of the world. Whoever follows me will never walk in darkness, but will have the light of life."*
> **JOHN 8:12**

Light Up the Night

Carol and I enjoy the winter months. One of the sure signs that winter will soon be upon us is the turning back of the clocks, going from daylight saving time to standard time. We enjoy this time of year because everything seems to slow down. We do not have as many chores that need to be attended to, as was the case when the sun would not set much before nine o'clock during the summer months. Now our evenings seem much longer, which gives us a chance to spend more time together. With lights on, we spend many evenings playing cards or putting jigsaw puzzles together.

You cannot measure darkness. Darkness is simply the lack of light. Though I live in a dark world, it is God's desire to draw me out of the darkness and to Him. Jesus said that He is the light of the world and that whoever follows Him will not have to walk in darkness.

Prayer

> *Thank You, Heavenly Father, for drawing me out of the darkness of the world. I am and will be forever grateful for the day the light of my soul was turned on through Your Son, Jesus Christ. Amen.*

OCTOBER 23

DAY 296

*So, if you think you are standing firm, be careful that
you don't fall! No temptation has seized you except what
is common to man. And God is faithful; he will not
let you be tempted beyond what you can bear.*
1 CORINTHIANS 10:12–13

Sitting Close to the Fire

When I have a campfire down at the cabin, I can tell how cold it is by how close everyone is sitting around the fire. The colder it gets the closer the chairs move to the fire ring. I read a book on bush pilots of Alaska where it got so cold, that even while they stood around a fire, if they did not turn around soon enough their backside would get frostbite.

If you stand too close to the fire, you take the chance of being burned.

It is my Heavenly Father's desire that I walk closely with Him. It is my goal each day to become a little more Christlike. That is easier said than done because the closer I get to God the more my adversary Satan is going to turn up the heat and try to make me to stumble. It is his desire to ruin my testimony.

Prayer

*Heavenly Father, protect me from being burned by temptation.
Help me to strengthen my weaknesses so that I will have victo-
ries each day over Satan's desire to break the fellowship that I
have with You. Amen.*

OCTOBER 24
DAY 297

For this reason I remind you to fan into flame the gift of God,
which is in you through the laying on of my hands. For God
did not give us a spirit of timidity, but a spirit of power.
2 TIMOTHY 1:6–7

Fan the Fire

Oxygen is what keeps a fire going provided there is fuel to be burned, such as wood, coal, gas, or oil. When you want to slow a fire down in a wood stove, you simply close the dampers, which cut off the oxygen supply to the fire. When starting a fire out at the campground, there are times when I have to help the process along by blowing or fanning the flames to ignite the wood around it. By doing this, you are forcing more oxygen onto the fire, helping it to burn better.

God wants me to burn brightly in a dark world. The Good News is God's oxygen for a lost world. It is my responsibility to fan the lives of people who do not know Jesus as their personal Savior with the gospel message.

Prayer

Dear Heavenly Father, help me to be the match that might
start the fire for someone who will in turn touch the hearts of
many for Your glory. Amen.

OCTOBER 25
DAY 298

The heavens declare the glory of God; the skies
proclaim the work of his hands.
PSALM 19:1

Hunter's Moon, Dog Star, and Milky Way

The full moon in October is called the "Hunter's Moon." If the night is clear when the full moon is out, it is so bright there are shadows from the light of the moon. Without the humidity of the summertime, the dry air provides a clearer observation of the night sky. The Dog Star is visible this time of year as it rises from the east twinkling with its full spectrum of colors, and I can see the Milky Way spreading across the sky.

Whenever I step outside, I always look up to see if the stars are out. On a perfectly clear night, I am mesmerized at the magnitude of their beauty. They truly do reveal the glory of my Creator and Heavenly Father.

Prayer

Thank You, Heavenly Father, for the order and beauty of Your creation. I am grateful for the reminder of yYur brilliance as I gaze upon Your handiwork in the night sky. Amen.

OCTOBER 26
DAY 299

Even when I am old and gray, do not forsake me, O God, till I declare your power to the next generation, your might to all who are to come.
PSALM 71:18

Killing Frost

My neighbor, who is one of the patriarchs of our community, says he has seen frost in all twelve months of the year. Since I have been here, I have seen frost in nine different months. Generally, I do not have to start scraping windshields until mid-October. Sometime during this month, I will look outside in the morning and the yard is white from frost. This frost brings to an end the growing season.

Some people think as they grow older and their hair goes from its natural color to frosty gray, their growing season ends. Retirement is not a work that you will find in the Bible. It is not God's desire for me at any age to stop growing spiritually. Actually, retirement should provide me with more opportunities to practice my spiritual gifts.

Prayer

> *Dear Heavenly Father, as I grow older and have more time to myself, help me to use this time wisely in a way to further Your kingdom here on earth. Amen.*

OCTOBER 27
DAY 300

"I am the good shepherd; I know my sheep and my sheep know me—just as the Father knows me and I know the Father."
JOHN 10:14–15

Applesauce

"An apple a day keeps the doctor away." For those of us who love apples, fall is a great time of year to enjoy the local varieties of home grown apples. Apples are the main ingredient for many delicious desserts. Some of my favorites are apple fritters, apple tarts, apple crisp, apple pie, and apple dumplings. Then there is applesauce. You have store-bought applesauce, friends' and neighbors' applesauce, my mom's applesauce, and my wife's applesauce. Not to hurt anyone's feelings, but hands down my wife's applesauce is the best. The texture and sweetness is just right. I could pick Carol's applesauce out of a line up of different applesauces.

Likewise, Jesus knows his sheep. I might be able to deceive my parents, spouse, friends, or minister into thinking I am a Christian but God truly knows my heart. I must never deceive myself into thinking I can fool God.

Prayer

> *Heavenly Father, I am grateful that You know and care for me. Help me to be a good fruit inspector and not to be deceived*

by those who claim to know You but have ulterior motives. Amen.

OCTOBER 28
DAY 301

For I am convinced that neither death nor life, neither angels nor demons, neither the present nor the future, nor any powers, neither height nor depth, nor anything else in all creation, will be able to separate us from the love of God that is in Christ Jesus our Lord.
ROMANS 8:38–39

Rain, Sleet, Snow, nor Freezing Rain

Neither rain, sleet, snow, nor freezing rain will keep the mail carrier from delivering the mail. That slogan is put to the test for our faithful mail carriers. Where I live in north central Pennsylvania, we get our fair share of mixed precipitation, and I can never remember a day when the mail was not delivered. I have an hour commute to my job. So far, I have been very fortunate in the seven years since I have lived here, I have not missed a day of work due to weather. Our township and state road crews are very generous when it comes to spreading cinders.

The world has many obstacles and distractions from keeping my focus on God. Even though I may get off track, there is nothing that can separate God's love for me. He loves me unconditionally and is patient with me when I fall short of His desires for me.

Prayer

Thank You, Heavenly Father, for loving me unconditionally in spite of myself. Help me to love others as You love me. Amen.

OCTOBER 29
DAY 302

So I say, live by the Spirit, and you will not gratify the desires of the
sinful nature. For the sinful nature desires what is contrary to the
Spirit, and the Spirit what is contrary to the sinful nature. They are
in conflict with each other, so that you do not do what you want.
GALATIANS 5:16–17

Call of the Wild

It is man's nature to like the feeling of being in control. When I get into situations where I have no say in the outcome, it makes me feel very uncomfortable. Then there is a part of me drawn to the unknown and I enjoy the adrenaline rush of not being in control. The call of the wild is something like this. Many individuals have left the comforts of home to explore the wilderness around them.

In my Christian walk, I have to be careful to keep the yearnings of my flesh in check. The desires of my flesh are a major target for my adversary to attack, to get me out of fellowship with my Heavenly Father. I need to remember, I am to live by the spirit and not by the flesh.

Prayer

> *Dear Lord, I pray that each day I hear Your calling for me.*
> *Help me not to be distracted by the lust of the flesh but to live*
> *each day by the desires of Your Spirit. Amen.*

OCTOBER 30
DAY 303

*"He who belongs to God hears what God says. The reason
you do not hear is that you do not belong to God."*
JOHN 8:47

Grouse

I am beginning my thirty-eighth year of hunting and I have never
shot a grouse. I never really pursued grouse in Lancaster County, where
I hunted for most of those years. Pheasant was our bird of choice to
hunt. After the decline of the native pheasant and our move to Sullivan
County, I began to hunt grouse more regularly. Grouse are fast when
flushed and seldom provide a good shot. My final excuse for never
shooting a grouse is that when I flush a grouse I am usually in thick
cover and I hear them but do not see them.

I accepted Jesus as my personal Savior when I was twenty-five years
old. Was that the first time I ever heard the gospel? No. Like many
people, I heard but I did not see. Even though the world is blind to
God's reconciliation, I still need them to hear the Good News because
I never know when the Spirit of God will remove their blindness and
see Jesus for who He is.

Prayer

*Help me, Heavenly Father, continue to be faithful in sharing
the Good News of the gospel with those who do not know You
because Your Word tells us that faith comes through hearing
(Rom. 10:17). Amen.*

OCTOBER 31
DAY 304

*And no wonder, for Satan himself masquerades as an
angel of light. It is not surprising, then, if his servants
masquerade as servants of righteousness.*
2 CORINTHIANS 11:14–15

Halloween

Views on how to celebrate Halloween are as many there are denominations in the church of Jesus Christ. When I was a young boy growing up in the early sixties, Halloween fell right in behind Christmas and Easter; for days I looked forward to it with anticipation. It was the one night of the year when I would go to my neighbors and return home with a bag full of big candy bars and sweet treats. It was a dream come true for any child. It was done innocently without the knowledge of any occult activity. I would dress up as a pirate, hobo, clown, and other make-believe characters hoping the adults could not guess who I was.

I need to be very careful of false prophets and teachers, who disguise themselves as Christians but truly have ulterior motives. Satan is the angel of light and is very good at dressing up as something that appears good but will cause me to stumble in my walk with God.

Prayer

*Heavenly Father, give me a discerning spirit. Help me to see
through our adversary's trickery. Help me to know Your Word
so I can pick out false teaching when I hear it. Amen.*

NOVEMBER 1

DAY 305

In addition to all this, take up the shield of faith, with which
you can extinguish all the flaming arrows of the evil one.
EPHESIANS 6:16

A Protective Barrier

Now came the time for some of the final touches on the cabin. The eaves along the side, the front, and the back of the cabin had large open areas for air to pass through. I decided to use insulation to seal these airways. The cabin roof is vented, so I was not worried about making the cabin too air tight. The insulation proved to be an effective shield from letting the cold winter air inside the warm cabin.

It is God's desire that my life is full of joy. Satan, on the other hand, desires to rob as much of that joy as he possibly can from my life. That is why I need to stay close to God, so that He will provide a protective shield from the wiles of Satan and his demons.

Prayer

> *Dear Heavenly Father, I pray I walk each day with You at my*
> *side to protect me from my adversary's attacks so my joy may*
> *be full. Amen.*

NOVEMBER 2

DAY 306

Blessed is the man who perseveres under trial...When
tempted, no one should say, "God is tempting me." For God
cannot be tempted by evil, nor does he tempt anyone.
JAMES 1:12–13

Irritable Insulation

Insulation is a wonderful building material. It keeps the heat in and the cold out. It can make a big difference in your heating bills if you do not cut corners when insulating your home.

When installing insulation I take some precautionary measures. That pink fluffy and soft insulation is really a cushion of fine glass fibers.

When working with insulation it is inevitable that some of these fibers will become airborne. I wear a mask so as not to breathe these fibers into my lungs, and I wear a long-sleeved shirt to prevent skin irritation.

Living a Christian life is a wonderful experience. That is not to say there will not be trials and irritations along the way. If I take precautionary measures, such as reading His Word and prayer time, God will use these trials to teach us valuable lessons to become more Christlike.

Prayer

> *Heavenly Father, I pray life's irritations will only strengthen my relationship with You, and reaffirm to me daily that You are in control. Amen.*

NOVEMBER 3
Day 307

Not one of all the Lord's good promises to the house of Israel failed; every one was fulfilled.
Joshua 21:45

Comfort in a Warm Cabin

It would be hard to heat the cabin in the dead of winter without insulation. I would have had to keep the drafts on the wood stove wide open to keep the fire burning as hot as possible to maintain a comfortable temperature. The cold air coming through the eaves would be lowering the temperature almost as quickly as I was trying to raise the temperature. After the cabin was insulated, I have no problem keeping the cabin warm. Even when the temperature dips below ten degrees, I can enjoy supper or read a book in the comfort of a short-sleeved shirt.

Fulfilled biblical prophecy gives me much comfort also. Throughout the Bible, those who know the true and living God were comforted by their Heavenly Father's faithfulness. His faithfulness reassures me in a deceitful world knowing He never breaks a promise.

Prayer

> *Dear Heavenly Father, I am grateful for all the fulfilled prophecies and look forward with anticipation to the promises yet to be fulfilled. Amen.*

NOVEMBER 4
DAY 308

"Therefore I tell you, do not worry about your life, what you will eat or drink; or about your body, what you will wear. Is not life more important than food, and the body more important than clothes?"
MATTHEW 6:25

Ease My Mind

The insulation is a very good protective barrier to keep the warmth in the cabin but it does little to keep animals out of the cabin. I was concerned that when the cabin was not in use, it would be very easy for squirrels, skunks, opossums, raccoons, and porcupines to move in. I saw the destructive behavior of red squirrels first hand when they chewed through the screening of our side porch and through the plastic container filled with sunflower seeds. I wanted to prevent that type of activity in an unsupervised cabin. I used chicken wire with inch-wide holes to seal every possible point of entry, so far so good. That was one less worry on my mind.

God promises to provide for my daily needs. Even though I know God is in control, my human nature takes over, and I find myself worrying over something that has not happened. God tells me each day has enough unknowns and I should not fret over things yet to come.

Prayer

> *Heavenly Father, I am truly grateful for all Your blessings in my life, from the breath You give me to the food I eat. Help me not to worry over things yet to come and circumstances out of my control. Amen.*

NOVEMBER 5

DAY 309

After that, we who are still alive and left will be caught
up together with them in the clouds to meet the Lord in
the air. And so we will be with the Lord forever.
1 THESSALONIANS 4:17

Protection from Destruction

Wherever there was a gap big enough for a red squirrel to get through, I stapled up chicken wire. I surrendered myself to the fact that keeping field mice out could not be accomplished. Mice I could keep under control with traps. I just did not want to open the cabin door and be greeted by the back end of a skunk. I have seen how destructive raccoons can be, and the red squirrels were trying to build living quarters in the bunk area even before the cabin was chinked. To date the chicken wire has proven to be a very effective barrier against the destructive behavior of my neighboring critters.

I am glad God is going to protect His church from the destruction during the tribulation period. I believe the rapture of the church will come before Armageddon. God will protect His church from the trumpet judgments and the seven bowls of fury spoken about in the book of Revelation.

Prayer

Help me, Heavenly Father, to reach as many people as I can
with the gospel of Jesus Christ so they too will be saved from the
wrath of the tribulation period. Amen.

NOVEMBER 6

DAY 310

Remember the wonders he has done, his miracles, and the judgments he pronounced.
1 CHRONICLES 16:12

Remembering Our Heritage

Sometimes when I am having a bad day, I think about the trials and tribulations experienced by the American settlers. I enjoy early American history. It is truly amazing the progress made from Independence Day to today. That being said, I am sometimes envious of the simpler life experienced by my ancestors. Life was lived at a slower pace and there was more time spent together with family and community. This is one of the reasons I enjoyed building the log cabin. It helped me to remember my heritage.

I have a rich Christian heritage also. All through Hebrews chapter eleven, it tells me about the great patriarchs of faith. It is good to remember the deeds they were able to accomplish through their complete faith in God.

Prayer

Dear Heavenly Father, help me to remember the great things You have accomplished through mere men. I pray I would be one of those faithful servants worthy to be used by You. Amen.

NOVEMBER 7

Day 311

Against you, you only, have sinned and done what is evil in your sight, so that you are proved right when you speak and justified when you judge. Surely I was sinful at birth,
Psalm 51:4–5

Getting Used to the Cold

Spring and fall are good transition seasons to give bodies a chance to become acclimated to the extreme temperatures of summer and winter. In the summertime, when the temperatures are averaging in the mid-eighties and it drops to the low sixties, it seems cold; but in the winter when we are averaging temperatures in the mid-thirties and we get a fifty-degree day, it feels warm. It takes me a month to get used to the change, but once I am accustomed to the warmer or colder temperatures, I feel comfortable.

I am born with a sin nature. It is my natural desire to sin and Satan is always ready to fulfill those desires. The world is very good at desensitizing my flesh to the evil around me. Before accepting Jesus, my conscience could not help me to decide right from wrong because I got so used to the morals of the world, I began to think they were right. Once I became a Christian, my eyes were opened and now it is hard to believe I never noticed the declining morals around me.

Prayer

Heavenly Father, I pray that I would never get used to the sin around me. Help me to keep my heart from being hardened by the world's declining values. Amen.

NOVEMBER 8
DAY 312

*And the prayer offered in faith will make the sick
person well; the Lord will raise him up.*
JAMES 5:15

Catching a Cold

As my body adjusts to the change in temperatures from summer to fall, it also seems I become more susceptible to the cold virus. Winter is known as the flu season. Fortunately, I can say I have never gotten the flu but I do catch the common cold. My symptoms usually start out with congestion of the chest, and then it works it way up to my sinuses until it clears up, usually in a two-week period. My remedy for the common cold is rest and the chicken noodle soup.

I am grateful that God is ultimately in control of my health. He is the "Great Physician." Along with doctors and medications, it is important for me to pray for God's healing touch. Prayer brings me the peace I need for my body to heal.

Prayer

*Dear Heavenly Father, thank You for each breath You give
me. In my time of illness let me never forget to come to You in
prayer. Amen.*

NOVEMBER 9
DAY 313

*If you, O Lord, kept a record of sins, O Lord, who
could stand? But with you there is forgiveness;*
PSALM 130:3–4

Indian Summer

During the month of November, we will get a week where temperatures creep back up to the seventies. We call this week of mild weather our "Indian Summer." I like to put up the Christmas lights during this stretch of warm weather. It is also a time when outside chores that have not been completed can be finished before it is too late, and the winter freeze is here to stay.

It is never too late to ask God's forgiveness. It might come late in one's life when their spirit is warmed up to God's love, and the seed of salvation through Christ can be planted before the heart is frozen solid.

Prayer

> *Dear Heavenly Father, I pray for all those adults who have yet to make a decision for You. I hope that hearts would warm to Your love so they can experience an "Indian Summer" of Jesus as their personal Savior. Amen.*

NOVEMBER 10
DAY 314

Do your best to present yourself to God as one approved,
a workman who does not need to be ashamed and
who correctly handles the word of truth.
2 TIMOTHY 2:15

Not Cutting Corners

Working six hours each weekend, the cabin took ten months or two hundred and forty hours to complete. I was very pleased with the result. It was the first time I had tackled a project of this magnitude. The older I get the more particular I am when fixing or building something. My motto used to be, "If it works it doesn't matter what it looks like"; now I want it to work and look good. For the sake of paying less or finding an easier way to do something, I am apt to take shortcuts. That was not the case when I built the cabin. Instead of a canvas tarp for a roof, I have a tin roof, and having a two-man loft for sleeping quarters was not in my original plans.

It is God's desire for me to do my best no matter what I am doing. He does not want me to take a shortcut on my own for the desired path He has for my life. If I am doing my best in both my physical and spiritual life, I can be sure God's plan for my life will be carried out.

Prayer

Help me, Heavenly Father, to do my best for You in every aspect of my life. Whether it is at work or at home, I pray I will please You. Amen.

NOVEMBER 11
DAY 315

How sweet are your words to my taste,
sweeter than honey to my mouth!
PSALM 119:103

Corn Bread and Molasses

I like cornbread warm out of the oven with butter melted into it. During hunting season, one meal I enjoy making is chili with cornbread. I use my ten-inch Dutch oven when making the cornbread. I mix up cornmeal, flour, sugar, milk, eggs and baking powder, and then I pour those ingredients into my lightly oiled Dutch oven. I put the lid on and put fourteen charcoal briquettes on top and seven on the bottom. After thirty-five minutes, I remove the hot coals, turn the oven over and the best tasting cornbread is on the lid ready to serve my hungry hunters. I always have molasses on the table to spread over the warm cornbread.

Psalms refers to God's Word as being sweeter than honey. I need a daily diet of God's Word in my life. The Spirit of God will continue to reveal new truths to me throughout my entire life. I can never deplete the knowledge God wants to share with me from His Word.

Prayer

Heavenly Father, I pray I would desire to fill my spiritual needs with Your words with the same desire I have to fill my physical appetite with delicious desserts. Amen.

NOVEMBER 12
DAY 316

Finally, brothers, we instructed you how to live in order to please God, as in fact you are living. Now we ask you and urge you in the Lord Jesus to do this more and more.
1 THESSALONIANS 4:1

Coffee (One of Life's Simple Pleasures)

I had my first taste of coffee when I was tall enough to reach my parents' coffee cup and dunk a cookie into it. I have been dunking all types of desserts ever since. Just the aroma of coffee is a pleasing experience. I remember going to the grocery store with my mom as a child. One of the things I looked forward to on these trips was when she ground the coffee beans, and a wonderful smell was emitted. For me, coffee is one of life's simple pleasures. It is pleasing to smell, tastes good, and warms me up on a cold winter's day.

It is my Heavenly Father's desire that I live a life pleasing to Him. What is most pleasing to God is my obedience to Him. If I keep Jesus on the throne of my heart and self on the cross, I will do well in living a life agreeable to God.

Prayer

Dear Heavenly Father, when I start using the word I—as in, "I like," "I want to do this," or "I think I'll do this"—remind me quickly before I spoil your brew, that it is not about me but all about You. Amen.

NOVEMBER 13
DAY 317

*All your sons will be taught by the Lord, and
great will be your children's peace.*
ISAIAH 54:13

A Place to Rest

Everybody needs a place to relax and unwind from the rigors of
everyday life. Where we live is such a place. Including our house, there
are twelve houses within a quarter mile of each other. Out of those
twelve, there are three permanent residents and nine houses used for
cabins. One of the reasons I moved to this area was so my children and
my grandchildren would have a place to go to get away from the stresses
of their daily lives without paying a fortune for a vacation. I built the
cabin for me in the pines for the same reason.

It is natural for parents to want the best for their children. I hope
that through our prayers and the example of living a Christian life, the
peace our children experience will be great.

Prayer

*Dear Heavenly Father, I pray that Carol and I will leave a
legacy behind for our children and grandchildren that would
teach them to give their lives to You so they can attain the
tranquility only You can provide. Amen.*

NOVEMBER 14
DAY 318

*You have made my days a mere handbreadth; the span of my
years is as nothing before you. Each man's life is but a breath.*
PSALM 39:5

Seeing Your Breath

When it is cold outside you can see your breath. The natural phenomenon occurs when the warm air from your lungs mixes with the cold air outside and condensation takes place. The visible cloud of condensation only lasts for a short time. The colder it is outside the more visible the cloud of condensation becomes and the longer it remains visible in the air. Seeing my breath while I am outside is a sure sign that winter's grip will soon be upon us.

Seeing my breath vanish right before my eyes is a reminder to me of the brevity of life. The book of James tells me my life is a mist that appears for a little while and then vanishes (James 4:14). Each breath I take is a gift from God and it should not be taken for granted.

Prayer

> *Heavenly Father, I pray that I will use the time You have given me wisely. "Today is the first day of the rest of my life." Help me to live each day as if it was my last. Amen.*

NOVEMBER 15

DAY 319

Dear friends, I urge you, as aliens and strangers in the world, to abstain from sinful desires, which war against your soul.
1 PETER 2:11

No Worldly Distractions

One of the reasons I enjoy living in the mountains is that it is free from worldly distractions. The more often I put myself in situations where I am weak to certain temptations, the more likely I am to stumble and fall into sin. The more often I open the cupboards with all the snacks, the more likely I am going to eat something in between meals.

The big city is full of lustful pleasures. I need to keep my eyes focused on the Lord. Lot's troubles began when he pitched his tents near Sodom (Gen. 13:12–13). Man's flesh is weak. So being near a constant barrage of activities wanting to fill these desires, it is no wonder people are continually falling out of fellowship with God.

Prayer

> *Thank you, Heavenly Father, for the opportunity to live close to Your creations free from man's distractions. I pray that those living in areas where Satan has a stronghold would keep their eyes on You. Amen.*

NOVEMBER 16
DAY 320

The sluggard craves and gets nothing, but the desires of the diligent are fully satisfied.
PROVERBS 13:4

Coffee Pot on Pulley

Above the wood-burning stove in the cabin, I have chains hanging down from hooks screwed into the support beam. On one chain hangs my two-quart pot with lid and on the other chain hangs the coffee pot. This works out well for regulating the heat. I can bring something to a boil by setting the pots directly on the wood stove or just keep something warm by keeping it about six chain links above the stove. For added convenience, I put the chain attached to the coffee pot through a pulley. Now, I can lower the coffee from the loft so there will be hot coffee when we come down for breakfast.

There is a difference between a convenience and being lazy. My dad always told us, "Just because you're poor doesn't mean that you have to live in a dirty house," I am sure we have all heard the saying "Idle hands are the devil's workshop." God's Word tells me that if I am lazy, I might lack in needed provisions. God does not bless laziness.

Prayer

Dear Heavenly Father, I pray that I find the correct balance between work and leisure in my life. Help me to do all I can with the health You have given me. Amen.

NOVEMBER 17
DAY 321

Without wood a fire goes out; without gossip a quarrel dies down.
PROVERBS 26:20

Without Wood a Fire Goes Out

When the temperatures drop below freezing, the cabin is comfortably warm on the inside when a fire is burning in the wood stove. The cabin is not insulated, so it does not retain heat from the wood-burning stove for a long period. So on those nights when the temperatures are below freezing, someone needs to get out of their warm sleeping bag to put a couple of logs on the fire to keep the cabin warm when we wake up and have our breakfast.

As charcoal to embers and as wood to fire, so is a quarrelsome man for kindling strife (Prov. 26:21). I have to be careful not to spread gossip. Once words leave my mouth, they cannot be retrieved. As my father would say, "Think before you speak."

Prayer

Heavenly Father, help my speech not to be full of idle words. Control my tongue; let my words be a blessing to those who hear them. Amen.

NOVEMBER 18

DAY 322

Share with God's people who are in need. Practice hospitality.
ROMANS 12:13

Sharing Your Blessings with Others

Each year for the past six years around this time, I have received a phone call from a friend of ours in Lancaster. He calls to check if Carol and I will be home the Sunday before the opening day of bear season. He comes up with his son and his grandsons to take their annual walk back to the state game lands. Before we take our walk, we will visit over a cup of coffee and catch up on family and church news.

I am only steward of what I have. It is God's desire for me to share my blessings with and offer my hospitality to others. It is a great way for me to open my doors and share the love of God. Sharing what I have with others just might open the door to sharing the gospel of Jesus Christ with my visitors.

Prayer

Dear Heavenly Father, I am grateful for all the blessings I have received in my life. Let me without hesitation share them with others. I pray my hospitality would lead others to knowing Jesus as their personal Savior. Amen.

NOVEMBER 19

DAY 323

But even if you should suffer for what is right, you are blessed.
"Do not fear what they fear, do not be frightened.
I PETER 3:14

Bears, Bobcats, and Coyotes

During the spring, summer, and fall of the year we bring in our bird feeders every night. The reason for this is to protect them from hungry bears that may be passing through under the cover of night. They love birdseed and have no problem destroying the bird feeders to get to it. When we leave our cock-a-poo out at night to do her business we turn on the floodlight to make sure there are no bears around.

I respect the bears, coyotes, bobcats and possible cougars that live in our woods but I do not fear them.

As a Christian, I need not live my life in fear. God is in complete control of my life as long as I am careful to remain in fellowship with Him. I never have to worry about the unexpected if I put my faith and trust in the Lord.

Prayer

Thank You, dear Lord, that I can live each day confidently and not in fear of what may come my way because You are in control of my life. Amen.

NOVEMBER 20
DAY 324

It teaches us to say "No" to ungodliness and worldly passions, and to live self-controlled, upright and godly lives in this present age,
TITUS 2:12

No Modern Conveniences

The cabin is only one hundred yards away from the house. The guys I work with think I am crazy for wanting to give up all the comforts of home to hunt out of a cabin lacking all modern conveniences. It is like stepping into a time machine and going back to the eighteenth century. I have often said, "I was born a couple of hundred years too late." I enjoy denying myself the modern conveniences of electricity and plumbing and all the benefits that go along with them.

The world would like me to take part in all the pleasures it has to offer. I need to deny myself the temporary satisfying activities of this world. As the book of Titus tells me, I need to say no to worldly passions and live a self-controlled, upright, and godly life.

Prayer

Each day, Heavenly Father, I pray that I will pick up my cross, so I can experience the full joy You wish for me to have in this lifetime. Amen.

NOVEMBER 21
DAY 325

Through him you believe in God, who raised him from the dead and glorified him, and so your faith and hope are in God.
1 PETER 1:21

Anticipation Growing

The holiday season is soon upon us. From Thanksgiving Day to New Year's Day there is added excitement in the air. There are more specials on TV, the stores are bustling with shoppers and foods we do not normally have the rest of the year are being prepared. I enjoy the holiday season. I enjoy the music, being with family and friends, the lights and the smells from baking to evergreens.

The Monday after Thanksgiving is also the start of buck season in Pennsylvania. I look forward with anticipation for this day. I can still remember those Sunday nights I could hardly fall asleep hoping to bag a buck the following morning.

What hope does anyone have not knowing Jesus as his or her personal Savior? I look forward with much anticipation to seeing Jesus face to face the day I walk through the doorway of death. No matter what comes my way, I always have hope in God.

Prayer

Thank You, Heavenly Father, for the hope You give me each day of my life. I awake each day knowing You are in control, and look forward with anticipation to how You may work in my life each day. Amen.

NOVEMBER 22
DAY 326

To the Jews who had believed him, Jesus said, "If you hold to my teaching, you are really my disciples."
JOHN 8:31

Passing on What You Know

The majority of what I know about hunting, fishing, and camping came from my days afield with my dad. I grew up in a hunting family, so I learned at a very young age what guns were used for, how to handle them, and to respect them. Dad taught me all that he knew about hunting whitetail deer, fly fishing, raising bird dogs and many other activities associated with the outdoors. Whatever he did not know he encouraged me to read up on. Now it is my turn to share all my knowledge with my nephew and his nephew.

It works the same for those who are further along in the walk with Jesus to disciple or mentor those who are just taking their first steps as believers. It is also God's desire I share my faith with those who need to hear the good news.

Prayer

Thank You, Lord, for the mentors You have placed in my life. I pray I have the wisdom to successfully disciple those in search of direction. Amen.

NOVEMBER 23
DAY 327

A perverse man stirs up dissension, and a gossip separates close friends.
PROVERBS 16:28

Hunting Stories

The word "exaggeration" is synonymous with fishing stories. An angler spreads his or her hands apart a little wider with each passing year when they tell their story of catching the big one. The same is true with hunting stories. This is the time of year cabins fill up and tales of outdoor adventures are shared with everyone who will listen. Racks get a little bigger, shots get a little longer, temperatures get a little colder, and the buck that was shot was moving a little faster. I enjoy listening to others as they share their outdoor experiences.

Sharing an unintentional exaggerative story of our outdoor adventures is harmless compared to gossip spoken in lunchrooms and over phones each day. Once words leave my mouth I cannot get them back. I have to be careful not to keep the rumor mill running when it gets to me. Gossip is never helpful to the one being talked about.

Prayer

> *Dear Heavenly Father, help me to stop gossip in its tracks. Give me the courage to stand up for the person being spoken about rather than spreading words that will tear them down. Amen.*

NOVEMBER 24
DAY 328

Preach the Word; be prepared in season and out of season; correct, rebuke and encourage—with great patience and careful instruction.
2 TIMOTHY 4:2

Preparations

Thanksgiving is a time of year for making preparations. Whether we call for reservations or buy all that is needed for our Thanksgiving feast, being prepared is the order for the day. A meal that only takes twenty minutes to eat takes days of preparation and planning.

This is also the time of year when I get ready for hunting season and the arrival of my nephew and his nephew. I make up the menu, buy groceries, pack my hunting clothes and equipment, and split the fire wood.

Being prepared is a good thing. God wants me to be prepared to share the Good News at a moment's notice. I never know when the door of opportunity may open to someone's heart that needs to hear about the love of Jesus.

Prayer

> *Heavenly Father, I pray I will always be prepared to be used by You. Help me to keep my life in order so my actions will support the words of Your Good News as I share them with others. Amen.*

NOVEMBER 25
DAY 329

Enter his gates with thanksgiving and his courts with praise; give thanks to him and praise his name.
PSALM 100:4

Favorite Holiday

My favorite holiday as an adult is Thanksgiving. Even as a child Thanksgiving was a day looked forward to with great anticipation. I could count the times Thanksgiving dinner was not made in the house I lived on one hand. I love the smells of all the foods as they are being prepared, onions being lightly sautéed in butter for the filling, pumpkin pies baking and the smell of the turkey slowly baking in the roasting pan emanating throughout the house. It is a time when family, friends, and relatives gather for a day filled with traditions. I always like to watch some of the Macy's Thanksgiving Day Parade to kick off the holiday season.

Thanksgiving is a day we set apart for giving thanks for the many blessings we enjoy in America. Truly, each day I need to be thanking my Heavenly Father for the countless blessing He provides for me daily.

Prayer

> *Thank You, Heavenly Father, for each breath I take and for restoring my relationship with You through Christ Jesus. To write everything down that I am thankful for without missing anything would be impossible. Amen.*

NOVEMBER 26
DAY 330

So then, dear friends, since you are looking forward to this, make every effort to be found spotless, blameless and at peace with him.
2 PETER 3:14

Sighting in the Rifle

When I first purchase a rifle, one of the first things I do before taking it hunting is to make sure it is sighted in. Being sighted in means the bullets fired from the rifle will hit the mark I am shooting at. Once sighted in I can shoot with confidence. Each year before I go hunting I make sure my scope has not been bumped and it is still shooting straight.

As a Christian, I need to hit my mark. The bulls' eye is Jesus Christ. The more I am a perfect reflection of Jesus the better I will be able to bring others to the saving knowledge of His death and resurrection. I continually make adjustments in my life to be sure my sights are on Jesus.

Prayer

> *Convict me, Heavenly Father, of any sin in my life, and help me to make any correction necessary to become more like Your Son Jesus Christ. Amen.*

NOVEMBER 27
DAY 331

But blessed is the man who trust in the
Lord, whose confidence is in him.
JEREMIAH 17:7

Picking a Good Spot

I enjoy taking long walks in the woods. I never leave the house without my compass when I go exploring the twenty-five thousand square acres of state game lands behind my house. With the compass, I have the confidence to travel in areas unexplored by me. I love to meander in woods where I have never been before. As I walk, I scout for turkey and deer sign for future areas to hunt. Finding a good spot to hunt gives me more confidence in actually seeing something when I go to hunting.

God never changes. God is love. God is all-forgiving. God is all-powerful and all-knowing. Jesus and the Holy Sprit are God. Knowing all of God's attributes gives me the confidence to go to Him for all of my needs. Walking through the scriptures and studying them gives me more confidence in living a victorious life for Christ in my daily travels.

Prayer

Thank You, Heavenly Father, for the trust I have in You. Help me to share Your attributes with others so they may experience self-assurance in You. Amen.

NOVEMBER 28

DAY 332

Even one of their own prophets has said, "Cretans are
always liars, evil brutes, and lazy gluttons."
TITUS 1:12

Over-eating During the Holidays

How often is this scene repeated in millions of homes across America each Thanksgiving: The men go back for second and third helpings and when done, they barely can walk to the couch where they fall asleep before the first half is over in the football game? I remember one time when I went to a smorgasbord and ate so much I was hardly able to stand up straight. I was a glutton that day and needed to ask for forgiveness. That experience taught me the lesson to eat just until I am full.

Gluttony is a sin and it truly can be deadly for anyone who makes it a daily habit. Our Heavenly Father promises to meet all of my physical needs each day. I try my best not to fill the desires of my flesh by overeating.

Prayer

Thank You, Heavenly Father, for meeting my needs each day.
Help me to eat in a way that would keep my temple in shape
for You to use for many years. Amen.

NOVEMBER 29

DAY 333

These stones are to be a memorial to the people of Israel forever.
JOSHUA 4:7

Date on Cabin

One of the wonderful aspects of being a Christian is the expectation each day brings. Each day is full of new opportunities to become more Christlike. I wake up most days with a good idea of what I want to do, but God may have other plans for me that change everything. With this said, I hope to have many years of memories down at the cabin. The cabin was built so that with a little annual maintenance it should be standing for many years to come. I built the cabin in the year 2005. I have chiseled the date into one of the logs so everyone will be reminded of when the cabin was constructed

I need to fill my mind with good and pure thoughts so my memories are pleasing to God. My memories are what build my faith in God. They are my testimony to all the wonderful things God has done in my life. Joshua was ordered by God to stack twelve rocks on the bank of the Jordan as a memorial for future generations, to remind them of the day the waters stopped flowing for their ancestors to cross.

Prayer

> *Dear Heavenly Father, help me to fill my mind with thoughts pleasing to You. I pray my life will be a memorial to all my family, friends, and acquaintances to how I faithfully walked with You. Amen.*

NOVEMBER 30
DAY 334

For we are to God the aroma of Christ among those who are being saved and those who are perishing. To the one we are the smell of death to the other, the fragrance of life.
2 CORINTHIANS 2:15–16

Yellow Birch

I was taking a walk in the woods with a friend, when he began to tell me about the article he read on the unique ability the bark of the yellow birch has to remain burning when lit. We collected some samples of the bark and returned to the cabin to put into practice what he read. Sure enough, when I lit the bark with a match it was like lighting the wick of a hurricane lamp. The oil in the bark that is extracted to make birch beer is the reason it burns so well. The fragrance emitted when burning birch wood is pleasing to the nose. My friend saves his birch wood to burn on holidays because the smoke from the chimney smells so good.

God says when I walk obediently with Him, I am the aroma of Christ. He also says I am the fragrance of life. During the holidays, many unsaved people make an exception from their usual routine by going to church. It is here the body of Christ needs to fill them with the delicate scent of life, so they too will come to know Jesus personally.

Prayer

Dear Heavenly Father, I pray that my daily walk would be a sweet aroma pleasing not only to You but to everyone I encounter each day so those who are not saved might be filled with the fragrance of life. Amen.

DECEMBER 1

Day 335

For this God is our God forever and ever, he
will be our guide even to the end.
PSALM 48:14

You Tag Will Drag, You Hookum Will Cookum

When I retire from my weekly job, I have entertained the idea of being a guide for hunting and fishing as a means of supplemental income. I could have guests stay at the Howling Wilderness Camp Friday through Sunday. I was thinking of targeting my clientele to pastors who need a getaway for a weekend. I would take them hunting and fishing, cook savory Dutch oven meals, and have fireside chats. Seeing as how I take walks almost every weekend, I could guide them into the woods to areas where they would be more likely to be successful and bring them out without getting lost.

God wants to be my guide in a lost world. After Jesus ascended into heaven He promised to send me the Holy Spirit to guide me in all that is truthful. With God's guidance, I will remain on the correct path of life.

Prayer

Thank You, Heavenly Father, for Your guidance in my life. Let me be sensitive each day to Your promptings for the direction You wish for me to go. Amen.

DECEMBER 2

Day 336

The apostles said to the Lord, "Increase our faith!"
LUKE 17:5

Building up the Wood Pile

I use wood as a supplementary heat source to help curb the cost of heating with propane. Making sure we have enough wood to get us through a winter is a yearly chore. I am always trying to increase my woodpile. Down at the cabin during hunting season, gathering kindling to keep the outside fire going when it dies down and splitting wood each day to make sure we have enough to get us through the night are two of our main chores. If the woodpile decreases, we have to increase our work.

John the Baptist told his followers, when it was time to baptize Jesus, that he needed to decrease and Jesus needed to increase (John 3:30). As I walk with Christ each day, my faith in Jesus should increase. In addition, the love I have in my heart for meeting the needs of others should grow larger.

Prayer

> *Dear Lord, I pray that I will become a little more like You each day. Let my faith in You increase my love for those who do not know You. Amen.*

DECEMBER 3
DAY 337

*Now faith is being sure of what we hope for
and certain of what we do not see.*
HEBREWS 11:1

Shooting Accurately

Just prior to deer hunting season, shooting ranges across Pennsylvania are crowded with hopeful hunters who want to make sure their firearm is shooting accurately. One of the first things I do when I get a new rifle is sight it in. Meaning, I will have the confidence the bullet will hit the spot where I am aiming. Whether I use a scope or open sights, I usually have to make adjustments to insure I am hitting my mark. The more I shoot my rifle and hit the spot I am aiming at, the more confidence I have in my rifle's accuracy.

The stronger my faith becomes, the surer I become that the promises of God are true. The more I am obedient and let God work in my life, the greater my belief becomes in all that I hope. As I walk with Christ, my confidence grows in all things unseen.

Prayer

Dear Heavenly Father, I am grateful for the hope and confidence You give me in knowing I will someday hit my heavenly target and spend eternity with You. Amen.

DECEMBER 4
DAY 338

You too, be patient and stand firm, because the Lord's coming is near.
JAMES 5:8

The Waiting Game

The first day of buck season, I like to leave camp early enough to get to my stand at least forty-five minutes before shooting time. This means I need to get up by three-thirty and break camp by four-thirty. I like to get to my stand early to be settled in so I have no reason for making any noise come sunrise. Once I am at my stand, the waiting game begins. It requires a great deal of patience to wait the many hours before possibly seeing what I am hunting for walk near my stand. There have been many days when I have sat in my stand from sunrise to sunset without seeing any more than squirrels and songbirds.

Father, give me the patience I need to endure the trials of everyday life. Let my patience open doors to opportunities for witnessing to others. Father, I am grateful that you are patient with me as I overcome weaknesses in my life.

Prayer

Heavenly Father, help me to use my time wisely, all through those times I am waiting for Your direction in my life. I pray that with each passing day I draw closer to You. Amen.

DECEMBER 5

DAY 339

But the angel said to them, "Don't be afraid. I bring you good news of great joy that will be for all the people. Today in the town of David a Savior has been born to you; he is Christ the Lord."
LUKE 2:10–11

The Love, Joy, and Hope of Hunting

Until the modern era of stockyards and butcher shops, hunting was an essential part of man's existence. There are still areas in the world where the family depends on the meat provided to them by the hunters in their family. More often than not when I go hunting, I come back with nothing. That is why they call it hunting and not killing. I enjoy all the aspects of the hunting experience: the hope of seeing what I am pursuing in a field, the joy of being successful, the love of being out in the peacefulness of God's creation, and sharing that experience with friends and family.

During this time of year we celebrate Advent, the coming of our Lord. We light a candle each week for four weeks. The candles represent the hope, joy, love, and peace I have for the coming of Christ. It is a wonderful time of year to remember the love God has for me and the eternal life I have through Jesus.

Prayer

Thank You, Heavenly Father, for Christmas. You truly are the reason for the season. Help me to celebrate Christmas every day so I may be a witness to someone who does not know baby Jesus. Amen.

DECEMBER 6
DAY 340

The Lord is good to those whose hope is in
him, to the one who seeks him.
LAMENTATIONS 3:25

Looking for Game

When I hunt for something, my main goal is to find the animal I am hunting. In some cases, hunting is synonymous with looking. Many tactics will improve my chances for a successful hunt. Being knowledgeable of the game or animal I am hunting for will greatly improve the chances of bagging my quarry. Knowing the area that I am hunting and preseason scouting for signs of the animal I am hunting will all help in finding the game I am seeking.

Man is constantly looking for new ways to bring pleasure into his life. However, there is a yearning in the heart of man that cannot be filled with worldly stuff. This hole can only be filled with the love of God. The more I know God by reading His Word, the Bible, or going to church, the greater my chances of finding what I really need to make my life complete and fulfilling.

Prayer

Dear Heavenly Father, help me to be an encourager to those who do not know You, to read Your Word and go to church. Use me to help unbelievers seeking to fill the void in their hearts make their hunt successful by finding Jesus. Amen.

DECEMBER 7
DAY 341

You will have plenty to eat, until you are full, and
you will praise the name of the Lord your God,
JOEL 2:26

Camp Cook

I started my cooking career as soon as I was able to reach the control knobs on the stove. My two meals of choice at that time were scrambled eggs and fried Lebanon bologna sandwiches. I guess having two older sisters and always being in the kitchen when Mom was baking led to my knowledge and enjoyment of cooking. No wonder I found myself being the camp cook. The wood-burning stove and Dutch ovens make cooking easier and add to the variety of meals on the menu. I enjoy providing tasty servings of food for my hungry hunters.

God promises to meet the daily needs of His saints. I have read several missionary stories where they received provisions in a very timely manner, when the results were out of their hands. Seek first the kingdom of God. If I do this, the Bible tells me that God will provide the necessities of life.

Prayer

Thank You, Heavenly Father, for meeting my needs daily. Help me to remain faithful in seeking the kingdom of God as my top priority in life. Amen.

DECEMBER 8
DAY 342

The true light that gives light to every man was coming into the world.
JOHN 1:9

In With a Flashlight, Out With a Flashlight

"In with a flashlight, out with a flashlight" is a saying we like to use in camp when we are hunting on the first day of buck season. This motto refers to the fact that we need to use a flashlight to find our deer stands in the morning and when we leave our stands, we need our flashlights to get back to camp. With the light from the flashlight illuminating our path, we can go as far into the mountains as we desire.

John the Baptist proclaimed that Jesus was the light of the world that was going to give light to every man. When Jesus appeared to His disciples following His resurrection He told them that He would send them the Holy Spirit to help them be witnesses for Him. He told them to be a witness from Jerusalem to the ends of the earth (Acts 1:8). With Jesus as my light I can go anywhere in the world and be an effective witness for Him.

Prayer

Dear Heavenly Father, I pray that distance or cultures would not prevent me from being the witness You want me to be. I pray that my light will shine brightly in a dark world. Amen.

DECEMBER 9
DAY 343

These things happened to them as examples and were written down as warnings for us, on whom the fulfillment of the ages has come.
1 CORINTHIANS 10:11

Busted

Any hunter who has hunted deer for several years has more than likely heard the warning signals of deer. It is a snort or whistling sound. Deer make this sound to alert one another to potential danger. It usually happens when I make a movement in my deer stand without realizing deer have entered into my area. After being busted, chances are all you will hear is the snort and then you will see white tails headed in the opposite direction.

Most animals have effective warning signals to help them survive their daily routines. God has not left man without warning signals to help him survive a lost world. Adverse consequences from sin experienced by others are an effective forewarning for me not to make the same mistakes. I need to be sensitive to God's warnings so that I stay clear of present dangers in a fallen world.

Prayer

> *Dear Heavenly Father, help me to be obedient to that small voice in my mind when it is telling me to change my course. Also, give me the courage to warn others to go in the opposite direction when they are in danger. Amen.*

DECEMBER 10
DAY 344

There is another who testifies in my favor, and I know that his testimony about me is valid.
JOHN 5:32

Reporting Back at Camp

One of the highlights of a hunting camp is when everyone returns in the evening after a long day's hunt. It feels good to stoke up the wood-burning stove and feel the warmth return to chilled bones. The cabin is a beehive of activity. I start the evening meal, dishes are done from the morning's breakfast, firewood is gathered, and hunting gear is put away. I usually have supper prepared within the hour. After thanking God for our food and a safe day in the woods, we begin to eat and tell each other what we saw. These conversations help to decide what we want to do the following day. Positive reports encourage tired hunters and boost the morale of the camp.

Going to church fills up my spiritual tank. Where I fellowship we have a time for praise and prayer requests. It is during this time I get a chance to hear how God is working in the lives of fellow saints. It is always good to hear the testimonies of others. It helps build my faith and encourages me to continue in obedience to my Heavenly Father.

Prayer

> *Jesus, I am grateful for the testimony You shared with the world on Your Father's behalf. I pray that my Christian walk will encourage fellow believers and the lost. Amen.*

DECEMBER 11
DAY 345

For all have sinned...but the gift of God is eternal life in Christ Jesus our Lord..."Everyone who calls on the name of the Lord will be saved."
ROMANS 3:23; 6:23; 10:13

Reflector Tape

Highways lead to country roads, which access dirt roads that go to logging roads, which eventually turn into paths in the woods. When I take walks, it is at the end of those paths when I get out my compass to make sure of the direction I am going. This is where I like to be in the woods. I never know what new things I will find or see for the first time. These hikes are very useful when it comes to knowing the terrain and scouting new areas to hunt. When I find a new place to hunt, I will use reflector tape and staple it to trees about twenty-five yards apart until I come to a path. When I enter the woods in the dark, the reflector tape brightens when the light from my flashlight hits it and guides me to the exact spot I want to be.

There are many roads to take in life, but only one road that leads me to the place where I need to be. In the book of Romans, there are verses that can be used to share the Gospel with someone that will lead them to the exact spot they need to be in their life.

Prayer

> *Heavenly Father, I pray You give me many opportunities to lead those who are lost down the Roman Road, so they will find eternal life with You. Amen.*

DECEMBER 12
DAY 346

But if from there you seek the Lord your God, you will find him if you look for him with all your soul.
DEUTERONOMY 4:29

Tree Stands

I have been hunting the white-tailed deer for thirty-four years. In all those years, I have only shot one deer with my feet on the ground. All the other deer were tagged from the vantage point of a tree stand. Being up in a tree stand gives me a three-fold advantage. One, the deer can't see me as easily; two, my scent is not a prevalent; and three, from the vantage point of a tree stand I can see the deer better because it gets me above the brush that limits my view if I were on the ground.

Many things in the world keep me from seeing the Lord effectively. Sin clouds my vision. The Bible tells me that if I look for the Lord I will find Him. I need to get above the daily distractions of everyday life so I can see God working in my life.

Prayer

> *Dear Heavenly Father, help me to see You in everything I do. Lift me up to give me the spiritual vision necessary to see the needs of others and the desire to meet those needs. Amen.*

DECEMBER 13
DAY 347

Jesus said to her, "I am the resurrection and the life. He who believes in me will live, even though he dies;"
JOHN 11:25

Waiting for the Sunrise

Deer hunting season with rifle begins the first Monday after Thanksgiving at sunrise. I try to get to my deer stand at least a half hour earlier than the shooting time listed in the hunting regulation book issued with my hunting license. This gives me time to get situated in my stand so I am done making noise when it comes time to hunt. I use the time before the sun rises as an opportunity to pray, stargaze, and nap. I always enjoy the transition from night to day especially when the sun rises in all its glory. The sun replaces the darkness with light and warms up the body.

Without the resurrection of God's Son, Jesus Christ, the Christian message would be futile. There would be no hope, no victory over death, and no eternal life. Jesus claiming victory over death is what proves He is the true Messiah. The Son of God replaces a dark world and fills it with light.

Prayer

Thank You, Jesus, for Your resurrection power. I am grateful for the hope I have each day, knowing the life I have through Your victory over death. Amen.

DECEMBER 14
DAY 348

Give us today our daily bread.
MATTHEW 6:11

Daily Provisions

Before we left to go deer hunting when I lived at home, my Dad would always ask, "Do you have your license, gun, and bullets?" If I forgot one of those three things, I could not go hunting. Of course, to make my hunting trip a more enjoyable experience there are certain provisions I would certainly want to have; such as a hot seat, warm clothes, rain parka, flashlight, knife, dragging rope, watch, boots, and gloves. When I go hunting from dawn to dusk, I pack in some snacks and drink as part of my daily provisions.

In the Lord's prayer, Jesus taught His disciples to ask His Heavenly Father to provide for their daily needs. "Give us this day our daily bread." God does not forget what I need each day and He will continue to provide those needs to me as long as I do not forget to remain obedient to Him.

Prayer

Thank You, Heavenly Father, for loving me enough to meet my daily needs. I pray that I will be forever grateful for the physical and spiritual bread You nourish me with each day. Amen.

DECEMBER 15
DAY 349

I will have mercy on whom I will have mercy, and I will have compassion on whom I will have compassion.
EXODUS 33:11

Clean Kill

Every year when I purchase a new hunting license, I receive a booklet explaining all the rules and regulations for the upcoming season— hours of the day when I can hunt, daily bag limits, restrictions on where I can hunt, what I can hunt, and what type of weapon I can use. There are some unwritten rules such as being courteous to landowners and striving to make a clean kill. Most hunters abide by all the rules written and unwritten, but as with any group of people there will always be a few that break the rules and hunt unethically. I never want to see an animal suffer after being shot.

It is not God's desire to see mankind suffer either. Suffering is a consequence of sin entering the world. Our God is a God of mercy and compassion. If I wait patiently on God, I will see His mercy and compassion in my life (Isa. 30:18).

Prayer

Dear Heavenly Father, when others experience suffering in their lives help me to be compassionate to them in a way so they will understand the mercy You have for mankind. Amen.

DECEMBER 16
DAY 350

We demolish arguments and every pretension that sets itself up against the knowledge of God, and we take captive every thought to make it obedient to Christ.
2 CORINTHIANS 10:5

Withstanding the Cold

The first day I can shoot a deer with a rifle is the Monday after Thanksgiving. Chances are the temperature is going to be somewhere below forty degrees. Most hunters get to their stands and try to remain as motionless as possible while waiting for a legal buck to walk within shooting distance. No matter how I dress to stay warm, withstanding the cold usually comes down to mind over matter. I can tolerate cold temperatures better than most hunters can. The colder the temperatures the better my chances are at getting a deer. The reason is that while I sit still other hunters are walking around trying to get warm, so hopefully they will move a deer my way.

The mind is also the battleground where I need to claim victory over temptation. I need to take captive every thought and make it obedient to Jesus Christ as God's Word tells us to do. If I do this, sin will not be able to penetrate my life and ruin the fellowship I enjoy with my Heavenly Father.

Prayer

> *Heavenly Father, I pray temptation would go no further than a passing thought. Help me to have control over my mind so I do not have to live with the consequences of sin. Amen.*

DECEMBER 17
DAY 351

"But your hearts must be fully committed to the Lord our God, to live by his decrees and obey his commands, as at this time."
1 KINGS 8:61

If I Had to Do It Over Again

As I look back on the past year, I can honestly say that my cabin building experience was everything I thought it would be. Everything I pictured mentally and the experiences shared with others at the cabin are just as I imagined. It was truly a dream come true.

If I had to do it all over again, I would put in bigger windows, make one of the sections of the roof with a transparent material to allow more daylight into the interior, and extend the ridgepole a foot off the backside of the cabin.

I wrote a song about getting rid of all the if's in my life. If I would have, if I should have, if I could have were some of the lyrics. When I live my life fully for God, that is to say, I consciously do all things to glorify Him, I do not have to worry about the results. He is in control, and whatever circumstances I face will be for me to become more Christlike. I do not have to wonder if I should have done something differently.

Prayer

> *Heavenly Father, help me to get rid of all the if's in my life by keeping self on the cross and Jesus on the throne of my heart. Amen.*

DECEMBER 18
DAY 352

The Lord God formed the man from the dust of the ground and breathed into his nostrils the breath of life, and the man became a living being.
GENESIS 2:7

Cleaning Up the Ashes Helps the Fire

After so many fires in the wood-burning stove or the fire ring, the ashes left behind from the burnt wood need to be cleaned. The harder and dryer the wood the less ashes you have remaining. Your different varieties of oaks, cherry and ash are good examples of hardwoods that leave a minimum of ashes after being burnt. I clean the wood stove out every two days of steady burning and the fire ring is cleaned out after five campfires. If I do not clean out the ashes, the ashes begin to smother the fire. Cleaning out the ashes helps the fire burn more effectively by allowing more oxygen to pass through the logs.

God created man out of the ashes and gave him life as He breathed into his nostrils. Out of the ashes from the destruction of the heavens by fire, God promises to create a new heaven and new earth for the righteous to live in (2 Pet. 3:12–13).

Prayer

> *Thank You, Heavenly Father, for creating me in Your image. I look forward to the day of living with You in the new heaven and new earth, where there will be no more sin or suffering. Amen.*

DECEMBER 19
DAY 353

In a loud voice they sang: "Worthy is the Lamb, who
was slain, to receive power and wealth and wisdom
and strength and honor and glory and praise!"
REVELATION 5:12

Cabin's Worth

The cabin turned out just as I imagined. It looked good and it was functional. Sometimes looks can be deceiving. Everything appeared to be in order. Only time and bad weather would reveal any flaws. The two main functions of the cabin are to keep the inhabitants warm and dry. I am happy to report that the cabin passed both of these tests wonderfully. To my delight, the cabin showed its worth in accommodating three hunters and their supplies. Sleeping quarters are comfortable and cooking meals on the wood-burning stove has proven to be easy and efficient.

Jesus was called the Lamb of God. He was perfect and without defect. He was worthy of sacrificing Himself on the cross for my sins. Revelation tells me He was worthy to open up the scrolls mentioned in chapter five. He proved His worth through His resurrection from the grave and defeat of death. Truly, there is no name under heaven more worthy of my worship than Jesus.

Prayer

Jesus, truly You are worthy of my complete surrender to You.
You love me, and only want the best for me. I pray my life will
help others know You personally. Amen.

DECEMBER 20

DAY 354

And God said, "Let the land produce living creatures according to their kinds: livestock, creatures that move along the ground, and wild animals, each according to its kind." And so it was.

GENESIS 1:24

Man's Best Attempt to Stay Warm

If humankind had to depend on what we were born with to stay warm, we would all be in big trouble. It would not be long until we would all be suffering from hypothermia. The truth of the matter is that even when we dress to stay warm, it is not long before we start feeling cold. I am sure some of us can remember when our mothers would bundle us up in a snowsuit for sledding and several hours later, we would return for some hot chocolate to thaw out. No matter how many layers of clothes I wear to go hunting, the cold temperature even without wind finds its way through.

While I am hunting or looking out the window from the comfort of my home on cold winter days, my thoughts often have me wondering how the wildlife can survive in such harsh conditions. The answer of course is God. God designed every creature with its own unique ability to survive in the environment it was born. When it comes to staying warm, man's ingenuity is no match for God's creation.

Prayer

Thank You, Heavenly Father, for revealing Yourself through Your creation. It is truly a testament to Your infinite wisdom. Amen.

DECEMBER 21
DAY 355

*"Remember the Sabbath day by keeping it holy. Six
days you shall labor and do as your work, but the
seventh day is a Sabbath to the Lord your God.*
EXODUS 20:8–10

Dad's Favorite Day

December 21st is the first day of winter. It is also the shortest day
of the year. Carol and I both enjoy the winter months. The days are
shorter and the nights are longer. There are not as many outside chores
so after supper we have more quality time to spend together. My dad,
on the other hand, enjoys the warmer weather and longer days. At this
point, you might be asking yourself why then would December 21 be
titled "Dad's Favorite Day" and not June 21, the longest day of the year.
Well, in my dad's way of thinking, each day after December 21 the days
start getting a little longer.

I consider every day to be a gift from God. I do believe, however,
there is enough biblical theology that tells me God wants me to set
aside one day a week to rest, meet with fellow believers and worship
Him. I am not necessarily a Christian just because I go to church, but
I will become a better Christian if I go to a church that believes God's
Word is infallible.

Prayer

*Dear Heavenly Father, I am grateful for the opportunity to
rest on Sundays and have the freedom to go to church and
worship You with fellow believers. Amen.*

DECEMBER 22

DAY 356

*For the life of a creature is in the blood, and I have given
it to you to make atonement for yourselves on the altar;
it is the blood that makes atonement for one's life.*
LEVITICUS 17:11

The Kill

For the past month, I have been writing about the many aspects of hunting enjoyed by a true sportsman. The pulling of a trigger to send a bullet in motion or the release of a string to send an arrow in flight is the final action the hunter takes before the hunted is killed. I hope that the skill of the hunter is at a level that will allow their shot to be true. When a clean kill is made only seconds pass before the life of the animal is gone.

Jesus was the perfect sacrifice. As Jesus hung from the cross, his life-sustaining blood dripped to the ground. There is power in the blood of Jesus. The blood of Jesus covers all our transgressions and purifies our hearts. God loved us so much he sent His only Son to die on the cross for our sins.

Prayer

> *Heavenly Father, You saved humanity from sin through the sacrifice of Your one and only Son. Thank You for the cleansing power of my Savior's blood, and let it be a constant reminder to me of the price paid for sin. Amen.*

DECEMBER 23

DAY 357

"I have told you these things, so that in me you may
have peace. In this world you will have trouble."
JOHN 16:33

Snow Is No Friend of the Deer

"It is snowing." That is all you have to say, and a schoolroom full of children will stop what they are doing to find the closest window to watch the white precipitation float gently to the ground. Without a doubt, snow is beautiful to look at and fun to play in. Snow is no fun to drive in and it is work to shovel out driveways. Snow is no friend to the deer either. Many of their food sources are covered and it is easier for hunters to track them. The white covering of snow on the ground works against their usually perfectly camouflaged brown bodies.

The world is no friend to Christians. The world is full of sin. The world's only desire is to fulfill the desires of the flesh with no regard to the feelings of others. The Christian has to be careful. I live in the world, but I am part of the kingdom of God. I need to minister to the lost while avoiding its many temptations.

Prayer

The world can be beautiful and fun to play in. I just pray that during my time here I will live in the spirit and not be controlled by the desires of my flesh. In Jesus' name, I pray. Amen.

DECEMBER 24
DAY 358

For it is time to seek the Lord, until he comes
and showers righteousness on you.
HOSEA 10:12

Keeping Track of Time

If you asked a hundred people to define time, you would get a hundred different answers. Webster even had a hard time defining time. There are over fifty different definitions for the word *time*. We measure time in seconds, minutes, hours, days, weeks, months, and years. We have watches, clocks, calendars, and even computerized pocket organizers to keep track of time. I use a watch when I hunt for several reasons. I like to document the time of day when I see deer, it helps me rendezvous with other hunters and it lets me get home on the designated time I tell my wife.

No matter how I keep track of time, one thing is for sure: I only have a certain amount of it. From my birth to my death, only God knows how many breaths I will take. The older I get the less I take each breath for granted. I want to live each moment for God's glory. I never know when it will be my last.

Prayer

Thank You, Heavenly Father, for each breath I take. Help me
to be a good steward of the time You have given me. I pray I
will use the allotted time You have given me wisely. Amen.

DECEMBER 25
DAY 359

Listen to advice and accept instruc-
tion, and in the end you will be wise.
PROVERBS 19:20

Listening to Experienced Hunters

Experience is an effective teacher. It just takes a longer time to learn and some of the consequences from bad experiences are irreversible in one's lifetime. This applies to every phase of life and it certainly applies to hunting. Listening to the good advice of experienced hunters will bring success much quicker than trying to learn everything on your own. The younger you are when you begin to listen to those who are experienced in whatever you may be pursuing, the more successful you will be in life.

Being successful in my Christian walk will also depend greatly on my willingness to accept Godly advice. Listening to the advice of godly men and women who have gone before will help me to avoid many pitfalls. Good advice is worth its weight in gold.

Prayer

Dear Heavenly Father, give me the wisdom to discern between
good and bad advice. I pray You would bring Godly people
into my life to share their testimonies with me, so I may learn
from their experiences. Amen.

DECEMBER 26
DAY 360

This will bring health to your body and nourishment to your bones.
PROVERBS 3:8

Don't Take Your Health for Granted

Each morning I wake up and thank God for the physical strength He has given me, and I consider it another chance to live more like Christ than the day before. Health is so often taken for granted. When I was younger, I did not consider the benefits of good health. I made several wrong choices, which became habits that are adverse to good health. Overeating, smoking, and drug abuse are some of the most common bad habits formed at a young age.

Each breath I take is a gift from God. Living a healthy life is a choice I make each day. Knowing that my body is the temple of the living God (1 Cor. 3:16) has helped me to break bad habits and start good ones. I make a conscious effort to treat my body in a way that would be pleasing to God.

Prayer

Dear Heavenly Father, I am humbled that You would choose man's body to be Your dwelling place. Knowing this helps me to make healthy choices in living out my life for You. Amen.

DECEMBER 27
DAY 361

Just as each of us has one body with many members, and these members do not all have the same function, so in Christ we who are many form one body,
ROMANS 12:4–5

Delegation of Camp Chores

In order for everybody to have the same amount of time hunting and time to sit around the campfire and relax, the camp chores need to be delegated. The three main chores are cooking, doing the dishes, and gathering firewood. This past hunting season we had three in camp including myself. I did the cooking, my nephew did the dishes and his nephew kept the firewood and kindling supplied. If everyone does his or her part, camp runs smoothly and no one person is overloaded.

The same is true of the church only on a much bigger scale. Jesus is the head of the church and all the members make up the body of the church. Every member is needed for the body of the church to be fully effective. Every Christian has his or her spiritual gift that needs to be used. There is no gift or member who is of less importance or more vital that another. Everyone is needed for the body of Christ's church to reach its full potential.

Prayer

> *Dear Heavenly Father, no matter if my gifts are noticed by others or not within the church, allow me to be faithful in fulfilling my part so the church will be the witness You want it to be. Amen.*

DECEMBER 28
DAY 362

Similarly, if anyone competes as an athlete, he does not receive the victor's crown unless he competes according to the rules.
2 TIMOTHY 2:5

Game Laws

Hunting is a privilege. Hunting in Pennsylvania is governed by the Pennsylvania Game Commission. Each year the game commission meets to decide whether to change or add any new regulations. All decisions are based on what is best for the conservation of the animals being hunted and the safety of the hunter. Unfortunately, there will always be unethical hunters who choose not to pursue game by the rules.

All through life, our lives are governed by rules. Whether they are rules set by our parents or some governing authority, we need to obey them or we will be punished. Even in sports or games that we play, there are rules to abide by. If there were no rules, there would be chaos. God's handbook for mankind, better known as the Bible, is full of mandates. If I abide by them, I can live in harmony with others and experience the full joy God intends for me to have.

Prayer

Heavenly Father, help me to live my life in obedience. Be quick to convict me when I go astray. Thank You for your instruction manual, the Bible, in helping me to live a Godly life. Amen.

DECEMBER 29
DAY 363

"Be still, and know that I am God"... Open my eyes that I may see wonderful things in your law... My dear brothers, take note of this: Everyone should be quick to listen.
PSALM 46:10; 199:18; JAMES 1:19

Deer Stands

There are three techniques for hunting deer. One is to still hunt, which is an oxymoron, because you are not staying still, you walk very slowly thorough the woods and stop frequently to scan for deer. Second, is to set up drives. Here you have several hunters stand in likely areas where deer will run when other hunters walk through a section of woods making noise. Thirdly, and my technique of choice, is to find a spot where you know there is deer activity and remain stationary while waiting for the deer to come to you. I prefer to be in a tree stand when I am using this technique. Whether you are on the ground or in a tree to be successful, you need to be still, patient and alert for noise and motion.

These are good traits to have in my Christian walk. Sometimes I am caught up in the business of life and I take my eyes off God. I need to make time in my life for being still and time to focus on my Heavenly Father. I need to be alert to the promptings of the Holy Spirit. I need to learn to listen to God's voice and Godly advice and I should be constantly looking for ways to serve others.

Prayer

Dear Heavenly Father, I pray my spiritual senses will be more alert than ever, so I may hear your voice clearly and be obedient in my service for You. Amen.

DECEMBER 30
DAY 364

When he received the drink, Jesus said, "It is finished." With that, he bowed his head and gave up his spirit.
JOHN 19:30

It Is Finished

Besides minor modifications to the cabin, such as a nail here to hold a coat, or a hook there to hang a lantern, the day came when the cabin was complete. It was a satisfying moment indeed. I always feel gratified when I set a goal and complete it. Now it was time for the final clean up, time to transform the cabin from a work area to an area of leisure. All of the tools used in the construction were finally returned from where they had been removed ten months ago. The tools were no longer needed; the cabin was finished.

I no longer need to offer blood sacrifices to my Heavenly Father for my transgressions. When Jesus uttered those final words on the cross, "It is finished," just before His death, He meant the payment needed for the transgressions of man's past, present and future had been paid. He has since returned to His heavenly home, while He awaits the arrival of faithful believers.

Prayer

Heavenly Father, I am forever grateful that Your Son completed the work You had for Him, so I may have fellowship with You. I humbly thank You. Amen.

DECEMBER 31
DAY 365

But as for you, continue in what you have learned and have become convinced of, because you know those from whom you have learned it,
2 TIMOTHY 3:14

Maintenance

When sin entered the world so did death and deterioration. If God's creation is susceptible to destruction with the passing of time, I can only imagine how the passing of time takes its effect on things made by man. Everything man made slowly deteriorates and depreciates. So it is with the cabin. Yes, the cabin was finished, but the upkeep and the annual maintenance was only beginning.

So it is in life. Many people spend all of their working days saving and planning for that day when they retire from work. Unfortunately, many retire from their walk with God during this time. Retirement is not a word found in God's Word. When Jesus said, "It is finished, " the church's work had just begun. I need to continue to work to further God's kingdom until He takes me to my eternal home with Him.

Prayer

Dear Heavenly Father, I pray that as I grow older the enthusiasm for being a witness for You would grow stronger. Though I am weak, He is strong. Amen.

TO CONTACT THE AUTHOR

Davescabin.com

Molly24@ptd.net

*In dedication to my wife for allowing me to fulfill
my dream of building a log cabin.*